THEOPHILUS TO AUTOLYCUS

Theophilus of Antioch

THEOPHILUS TO AUTOLYCUS

Theophilus of Antioch

THEOPHILUS TO AUTOLYCUS
Theophilus of Antioch

© Lighthouse Publishing 2018
Theophilus of Antioch (c. 115 – c. 181)
Translated by: Rev. Marcus Dods (1834 – 1909)
Revised by: A.M. Overett (b. 1960)

All rights reserved. Without limiting the rights under copyright reserved above, no part of this publication may be reproduced, stored in a retrieval system, or transmitted, in any form or by any means (electronic, mechanical, photocopying, recording or otherwise), without the prior written permission of the copyright owner of this book.

Published by
Lighthouse Christian Publishing
SAN 257-4330
5531 Dufferin Drive
Savage, Minnesota, 55378
United States of America

www.lighthousechristianpublishing.com

Lighthouse Early Church Fathers

Introductory Note
TO THEOPHILUS OF ANTIOCH.

[A.d. 115–168–181.] Eusebius praises the pastoral fidelity of the primitive pastors, in their unwearied labors to protect their flocks from the heresies with which Satan contrived to endanger the souls of believers. By exhortations and admonitions, and then again by *oral discussions* and refutations, contending with the heretics themselves, they were prompt to ward off the devouring beasts from the fold of Christ. Such is the praise due to Theophilus, in his opinion; and he cites especially his lost work against Marcion as "of no mean character." He was one of the earliest commentators upon the Gospels, if not the first; and he seems to have been the earliest Christian historian of the Church of the Old Testament. His only remaining work, here presented, seems to have originated in an "oral discussion," such as Eusebius instances. But nobody seems to accord him due praise as the founder of the science of *Biblical Chronology* among Christians, save that his great successor in modern times, Abp. Usher, has not forgotten to pay him this tribute in the *Prolegomena* of his Annals.

Theophilus occupies an interesting position, after Ignatius, in the succession of faithful men who represented Barnabas and other prophets and teachers of Antioch, in that ancient seat, from which comes our name as Christians. I cannot forbear another reference to those recent authors who have so brilliantly illustrated and depicted the Antioch of the early Christians; because, if we wish to understand Autolycus,

1

we must *feel* the state of society which at once fascinated him, and disgusted Theophilus. The Fathers are dry to those only who lack imagination to reproduce their age, or who fail to study them geographically and chronologically. Besides this, one should bring to the study of their works, that sympathy springing from a burning love to Christ, which borrows its motto, in slightly altered words, from the noble saying of the African poet: "I am a *Christian*, and nothing which concerns *Christianity* do I consider foreign to myself."

Theophilus comes down to us only as an apologist intimately allied in spirit to Justin and Irenæus; and he should have been placed with Tatian between these two, in our series, had not the inexorable laws of our compilation brought them into this volume. I need add no more to what follows from the translator, save only the expression of a hope that others will enjoy this author as I do, rating him very highly, even at the side of Athenagoras. He is severe, yet gentle too, in dealing with his antagonist; and he cannot be charged with a more sublime contempt for heathenism than St. Paul betrays in all his writings, abjuring even Plato and Socrates, and accentuating his maxim, "The world by wisdom knew not God."
For him it was *Christ* to live; and I love Theophilus for this very fault, if it be such. He was of Antioch; and was content to be, simply and altogether, nothing but a Christian. The following is the original Introductory Notice—:

Little is known of the personal history of Theophilus of Antioch. We gather from the following treatise that he was born a pagan, and owed his conversion to Christianity to the careful study of the Holy Scriptures. Eusebius (*Hist. Eccl.*, iv. 20) declares that he was the sixth bishop of Antioch in Syria from the apostles, the names of his supposed predecessors being Eros, Cornelius, Hero, Ignatius, and Euodius. We also learn from the same writer, that Theophilus succeeded to the bishopric of Antioch in the eighth year of the reign of Marcus Aurelius, that is, in a.d. 168. He is related to have died either in a.d. 181, or in a.d. 188; some assigning him an episcopate of thirteen, and others of twenty-one, years.

Theophilus is said by Eusebius, Jerome, and others, to have written several works against the heresies which prevailed in his day. He himself refers in the following treatise to another of his compositions. Commentaries on the Gospels, arranged in the form of a harmony, and on the Book of Proverbs, are also ascribed to him by Jerome; but the sole remaining specimen of his writings consists of the three books that follow, addressed to his friend Autolycus. The occasion which called these forth is somewhat doubtful. It has been thought that they were written in refutation of a work which Autolycus had published against Christianity; but the more probable opinion is, that they were drawn forth by disparaging remarks made in conversation. The language of the writer leads to this conclusion.

In handling his subject, Theophilus goes over much the same ground as Justin Martyr and the rest of the early apologists. He is somewhat fond of fanciful interpretations of Scripture; but he evidently had a profound acquaintance with the inspired writings, and he powerfully exhibits their immense superiority in every respect over the heathen poetry and philosophy. The whole treatise was well fitted to lead on an intelligent pagan to the cordial acceptance of Christianity.

[I venture to assign to Theophilus a conjectural date of birth, *circiter* a.d. 115.4]

THEOPHILUS TO AUTOLYCUS

CHAPTER I.—AUTOLYCUS AN IDOLATER AND SCORNER OF CHRISTIANS.

A fluent tongue and an elegant style afford pleasure and such praise as vainglory delights in, to wretched men who have been corrupted in mind; the lover of truth does not give heed to ornamented speeches, but examines the real matter of the speech, what it is, and what kind it is. Since, then, my friend, you have assailed me with empty words, boasting of your gods of wood and stone, hammered and cast, carved and graven, which neither see nor hear, for they are idols, and the works of men's hands; and since, besides, you call me a Christian, as if this were a damning name to bear, I, for my part, avow that I am a Christian, and bear this name beloved of God, hoping to be serviceable to God. For it is not the case, as you suppose, that the name of God is hard to bear; but possibly you entertain this opinion of God, because you are yourself yet unserviceable to Him.

CHAPTER II.—THAT THE EYES OF THE SOUL MUST BE PURGED ERE GOD CAN BE SEEN.

But if you say, "Show me thy God," I would reply, "Show me yourself, and I will show you my God." Show, then, that the eyes of your soul are capable of seeing, and the ears of your heart able to hear; for as those who look with the eyes of the body perceive earthly objects and what concerns this life, and discriminate at the same time between things that differ, whether light or darkness, white or black, deformed or beautiful, well-proportioned and symmetrical or disproportioned and awkward, or monstrous or mutilated; and as in like manner also, by the sense of hearing, we discriminate either sharp, or deep, or sweet sounds; so the same holds good regarding the eyes of the soul and the ears of the heart, that it is by them we are able to behold God. For God is seen by those who are enabled to see Him when they have the eyes of their soul opened: for all have eyes; but in some they are overspread, and do not see the light of the sun. Yet it does not follow, because the blind do not see, that the light of the sun does not shine; but let the blind blame themselves and their own eyes. So also thou, O man, hast the eyes of thy soul overspread by thy sins and evil deeds. As a burnished mirror, so ought man to have his soul pure. When there is rust on the mirror, it is not possible that a man's face be seen in the mirror; so also when there is sin in a man, such a man cannot behold God. Do you, therefore, show me yourself, whether you are not an adulterer, or a fornicator, or a thief, or a robber, or a purloiner; whether you do not corrupt boys; whether you are not insolent, or a slanderer, or passionate, or envious, or proud, or supercilious; whether you are not a brawler, or covetous, or disobedient to parents; and whether you do not sell your children; for to those who do these things God is not manifest, unless they have first cleansed themselves from all impurity. All these things, then, involve you in darkness, as when a filmy defluxion on the eyes prevents one from beholding the light of the sun: thus also do iniquities, man, involve you in darkness, so that you cannot see God.

CHAPTER III.—NATURE OF GOD.

You will say, then, to me, "Do you, who see God, explain to me the appearance of God." Hear, O man. The appearance of God is ineffable and indescribable, and cannot be seen by eyes of flesh. For in glory He is incomprehensible, in greatness unfathomable, in height inconceivable, in power incomparable, in wisdom unrivalled, in goodness inimitable, in kindness unutterable. For if I say He is Light, I name but His own work; if I call Him Word, I name but His sovereignty; if I call Him Mind, I speak but of His wisdom; if I say He is Spirit, I speak of His breath; if I call Him Wisdom, I speak of His offspring; if I call Him Strength, I speak of His sway; if I call Him Power, I am mentioning His activity; if Providence,

I but mention His goodness; if I call Him Kingdom, I but mention His glory; if I call Him Lord, I mention His being judge; if I call Him Judge, I speak of Him as being just; if I call Him Father, I speak of all things as being from Him; if I call Him Fire, I but mention His anger. You will say, then, to me, "Is God angry?" Yes; He is angry with those who act wickedly, but He is good, and kind, and merciful, to those who love and fear Him; for He is a chastener of the godly, and father of the righteous; but he is a judge and punisher of the impious.

CHAPTER IV.—ATTRIBUTES OF GOD.

And He is without beginning, because He is unbegotten; and He is unchangeable, because He is immortal. And he is called God [Θεός] on account of His having placed [τεθεικέναι] all things on security afforded by Himself; and on account of [θέειν], for θέειν means running, and moving, and being active, and nourishing, and foreseeing, and governing, and making all things alive. But he is Lord, because He rules over the universe; Father, because he is before all things; Fashioner and Maker, because He is creator and maker of the universe; the Highest, because of His being above all; and Almighty, because He Himself rules and embraces all. For the heights of heaven, and the depths of the abysses, and the ends of the earth, are in His hand, and there is no place of His rest. For the heavens are His work, the earth is His creation, the sea is His handiwork; man is His formation and His image; sun, moon, and stars are His elements, made for signs, and seasons, and days, and years, that they may serve and be slaves to man; and all things God has made out of things that were not into things that are, in order that through His works His greatness may be known and understood.

CHAPTER V.—THE INVISIBLE GOD PERCEIVED THROUGH HIS WORKS.

For as the soul in man is not seen, being invisible to men, but is perceived through the motion of the body, so God cannot indeed be seen by human eyes, but is beheld and perceived through His providence and works. For, in like manner, as any person, when he sees a ship on the sea rigged and in sail, and making for the harbor, will no doubt infer that there is a pilot in her who is steering her; so we must perceive that God is the governor [pilot] of the whole universe, though He be not visible to the eyes of the flesh, since He is incomprehensible. For if a man cannot look upon the sun, though it be a very small heavenly body, on account of its exceeding heat and power, how shall not a mortal man be much more unable to face the glory of God, which is unutterable? For as the pomegranate, with the rind containing it, has within it many cells and compartments which are separated by tissues, and has also many seeds dwelling in it, so the whole creation is contained by the spirit of God, and the containing spirit is along with the creation contained by the hand of God. As, therefore, the seed of the pomegranate, dwelling inside, cannot see what is outside the rind, itself being within; so neither can man, who along with the whole creation is enclosed by the hand of God, behold God. Then again, an earthly king is believed to exist, even though he be not seen by all; for he is recognized by his laws and ordinances, and authorities, and forces, and statues; and are you unwilling that God should be recognized by His works and mighty deeds?

CHAPTER VI.—GOD IS KNOWN BY HIS WORKS.

Consider, O man, His works,—the timely rotation of the seasons, and the changes of temperature; the regular march of the stars; the well-ordered course of days and nights, and months, and years; the various beauty of seeds, and plants, and fruits; and the divers species of quadrupeds, and birds, and reptiles, and fishes, both of the rivers and of the sea; or consider the instinct implanted in these animals to beget and rear offspring, not for their own profit, but for the use of man;

and the providence with which God provides nourishment for all flesh, or the subjection in which He has ordained that all things subserve mankind. Consider, too, the flowing of sweet fountains and never-failing rivers, and the seasonable supply of dews, and showers, and rains; the manifold movement of the heavenly bodies, the morning star rising and heralding the approach of the perfect luminary; and the constellation of Pleiades, and Orion, and Arcturus, and the orbit of the other stars that circle through the heavens, all of which the manifold wisdom of God has called by names of their own. He is God alone who made light out of darkness, and brought forth light from His treasures, and formed the chambers of the south wind, and the treasure-houses of the deep, and the bounds of the seas, and the treasuries of snows and hail-storms, collecting the waters in the storehouses of the deep, and the darkness in His treasures, and bringing forth the sweet, and desirable, and pleasant light out of His treasures; "who causeth the vapors to ascend from the ends of the earth: He maketh lightnings for the rain;" who sends forth His thunder to terrify, and foretells by the lightning the peal of the thunder, that no soul may faint with the sudden shock; and who so moderates the violence of the lightning as it flashes out of heaven, that it does not consume the earth; for, if the lightning were allowed all its power, it would burn up the earth; and were the thunder allowed all its power, it would overthrow all the works that are therein.

CHAPTER VII.—WE SHALL SEE GOD WHEN WE PUT ON IMMORTALITY.

This is my God, the Lord of all, who alone stretched out the heaven, and established the breadth of the earth under it; who stirs the deep recesses of the sea, and makes its waves roar; who rules its power, and stills the tumult of its waves; who founded the earth upon the waters, and gave a spirit to nourish it; whose breath giveth light to the whole, who, if He withdraw His breath, the whole will utterly fail. By Him you speak, O man; His breath you breathe yet Him you know not. And this is your condition, because of the blindness of your soul, and the hardness of your heart. But, if you will, you may be healed. Entrust yourself to the Physician, and He will couch the eyes of your soul and of your heart. Who is the Physician? God, who heals and makes alive through His word and wisdom. God by His own word and wisdom made all things; for "by His word were the heavens made, and all the host of them by the breath of His mouth." Most excellent is His wisdom. By His wisdom God founded the earth; and by knowledge He prepared the heavens; and by understanding were the fountains of the great deep broken up, and the clouds poured out their dews. If thou perceivest these things, O man, living chastely, and holily, and righteously, thou canst see God. But before all let faith and the fear of God have rule in thy heart, and then shalt thou understand these things. When thou shalt have put off the mortal, and put on incorruption, then shall thou see God worthily. For God will raise thy flesh immortal with thy soul; and then, having become immortal, thou shalt see the Immortal, if now you believe on Him; and then you shall know that you have spoken unjustly against Him.

CHAPTER VIII.—FAITH REQUIRED IN ALL MATTERS.

But you do not believe that the dead are raised. When the resurrection shall take place, then you will believe, whether you will or no; and your faith shall be reckoned for unbelief, unless you believe now. And why do you not believe? Do you not know that faith is the leading principle in all matters? For what husbandman can reap, unless he first trust his seed to the earth? Or who can cross the sea, unless he first entrust himself to the boat and the pilot? And what sick person can be healed, unless first he trust himself to the care of the physician? And what art or knowledge can anyone learn, unless he first apply and entrust himself to the teacher? If, then, the husbandman trusts the earth, and the sailor the boat, and the sick the physician, will you not place confidence in God, even when you hold so many pledges at His hand? For first He created you out of nothing, and brought you into existence (for if your father was not, nor your mother, much more were you yourself at one time not in being), and formed you out of a small and moist substance, even out of the least drop, which at one time had itself no being; and God introduced you into this life. Moreover, you believe that the images made by men are gods, and do great things; and can you not believe that the God who made you is able also to make you afterwards?

CHAPTER IX.—IMMORALITIES OF THE GODS.

And, indeed, the names of those whom you say you worship, are the names of dead men. And these, too, who and what kind of men were they? Is not Saturn found to be a cannibal, destroying and devouring his own children? And if you name his son Jupiter, hear also his deeds and conduct—first, how he was suckled by a goat on Mount Ida, and having slain it, according to the myths, and flayed it, he made himself a coat of the hide. And his other deeds,—his incest, and adultery, and lust,—will be better recounted by Homer and the rest of the poets. Why should I further speak of his sons? How Hercules burnt himself; and about the drunk and raging Bacchus; and of Apollo fearing and fleeing from Achilles, and falling in love with Daphne, and being unaware of the fate of Hyacinthus; and of Venus wounded, and of Mars, the pest of mortals; and of the ichor flowing from the so-called gods.

And these, indeed, are the milder kinds of legends; since the god who is called Osiris is found to have been torn limb from limb, whose mysteries are celebrated annually, as if he had perished, and were being found, and sought for limb by limb. For neither is it known whether he perished, nor is it shown whether he is found. And why should I speak of Atys mutilated, or of Adonis wandering in the wood, and wounded by a boar while hunting; or of Æsculapius struck by a thunderbolt; or of the fugitive Serapis chased from Sinope to

Alexandria; or of the Scythian Diana, herself, too, a fugitive, and a homicide, and a huntress, and a passionate lover of Endymion? Now, it is not we who publish these things, but your own writers and poets.

CHAPTER X.—ABSURDITIES OF IDOLATRY.

Why should I further recount the multitude of animals worshipped by the Egyptians, both reptiles, and cattle, and wild beasts, and birds, and river-fishes; and even wash-pots and disgraceful noises? But if you cite the Greeks and the other nations, they worship stones and wood, and other kinds of material substances,—the images, as we have just been saying, of dead men. For Phidias is found in Pisa making for the Eleians the Olympian Jupiter, and at Athens the Minerva of the Acropolis. And I will inquire of you, my friend, how many Jupiters exist. For there is, firstly, Jupiter surnamed Olympian, then Jupiter Latiaris, and Jupiter Cassius, and Jupiter Tonans, and Jupiter Propator, and Jupiter Pannychius, and Jupiter Poliuchus, and Jupiter Capitolinus; and that Jupiter, the son of Saturn, who is king of the Cretans, has a tomb in Crete, but the rest, possibly, were not thought worthy of tombs. And if you speak of the mother of those who are called gods, far be it from me to utter with my lips her deeds, or the deeds of those by whom she is worshipped (for it is unlawful for us so much as to name such things), and what vast taxes and revenues she and her sons furnish to the king. For these are not gods, but idols, as we have already said, the works of men's hands and unclean demons. And such may all those become who make them and put their trust in them!

CHAPTER XI.—THE KING TO BE HONOURED, GOD TO BE WORSHIPPED.

Wherefore I will rather honor the king [than your gods], not, indeed, worshipping him, but praying for him. But God, the living and true God, I worship, knowing that the king is made by Him. You will say, then, to me, "Why do you not worship the king?" Because he is not made to be worshipped, but to be reverenced with lawful honor, for he is not a god, but a man appointed by God, not to be worshipped, but to judge justly. For in a kind of way his government is committed to him by God: as He will not have those called kings whom He has appointed under Himself; for "king" is his title, and it is not lawful for another to use it; so neither is it lawful for any to be worshipped but God only. Wherefore, O man, you are wholly in error. Accordingly, honor the king, be subject to him, and pray for him with loyal mind; for if you do this, you do the will of God. For the law that is of God, says, "My son, fear thou the Lord and the king, and be not disobedient to them; for suddenly they shall take vengeance on their enemies."

CHAPTER XII.—MEANING OF THE NAME CHRISTIAN.

And about your laughing at me and calling me "Christian," you know not what you are saying. First, because that which is anointed is sweet and serviceable, and far from contemptible. For what ship can be serviceable and seaworthy, unless it be first caulked [anointed]? Or what castle or house is beautiful and serviceable when it has not been anointed? And what man, when he enters into this life or into the gymnasium, is not anointed with oil? And what work has either ornament or beauty unless it be anointed and burnished? Then the air and all that is under heaven is in a certain sort anointed by light and spirit; and are you unwilling to be anointed with the oil of God? Wherefore we are called Christians on this account, because we are anointed with the oil of God.

CHAPTER XIII.—THE RESURRECTION PROVED BY EXAMPLES.

Then, as to your denying that the dead are raised—for you say, "Show me even one who has been raised from the dead, that seeing I may believe,"—first, what great thing is it if you believe when you have seen the thing done? Then, again, you believe that Hercules, who burned himself, lives; and that

Æsculapius, who was struck with lightning, was raised; and do you disbelieve the things that are told you by God? But, suppose I should show you a dead man raised and alive, even this you would disbelieve. God indeed exhibits to you many proofs that you may believe Him. For consider, if you please, the dying of seasons, and days, and nights, how these also die and rise again. And what? Is there not a resurrection going on of seeds and fruits, and this, too, for the use of men? A seed of wheat, for example, or of the other grains, when it is cast into the earth, first dies and rots away, then is raised, and becomes a stalk of corn. And the nature of trees and fruit-trees,—is it not that according to the appointment of God they produce their fruits in their seasons out of what has been unseen and invisible? Moreover, sometimes also a sparrow or some of the other birds, when in drinking it has swallowed a seed of apple or fig, or something else, has come to some rocky hillock or tomb, and has left the seed in its droppings, and the seed, which was once swallowed, and has passed though so great a heat, now striking root, a tree has grown up. And all these things does the wisdom of God effect, in order to manifest even by these things, that God is able to effect the general resurrection of all men. And if you would witness a more wonderful sight, which may prove a resurrection not only of earthly but of heavenly bodies, consider the resurrection of the moon, which occurs monthly; how it wanes, dies, and rises again. Hear further, O man, of the work of resurrection going on in yourself, even though you are unaware of it. For perhaps you have sometimes fallen sick, and lost flesh, and strength, and beauty; but when you received again from God mercy and healing, you picked up again in flesh and appearance, and recovered also your strength. And as you do not know where your flesh went away and disappeared to, so neither do you know whence it grew, Or whence it came again. But you will say, "From meats and drinks changed into blood." Quite so; but this, too, is the work of God, who thus operates, and not of any other.

CHAPTER XIV.—THEOPHILUS AN EXAMPLE OF CONVERSION.

Therefore, do not be skeptical, but believe; for I myself also used to disbelieve that this would take place, but now, having taken these things into consideration, I believe. At the same time, I met with the sacred Scriptures of the holy prophets, who also by the Spirit of God foretold the things that have already happened, just as they came to pass, and the things now occurring as they are now happening, and things future in the order in which they shall be accomplished. Admitting, therefore, the proof which events happening as predicted afford, I do not disbelieve, but I believe, obedient to God, whom, if you please, do you also submit to, believing Him, lest if now you continue unbelieving, you be convinced hereafter, when you are tormented with eternal punishments; which punishments, when they had been foretold by the prophets, the later-born poets and philosophers stole from the holy Scriptures, to make their doctrines worthy of credit. Yet these also have spoken beforehand of the punishments that are to light upon the profane and unbelieving, in order that none be left without a witness, or be able to say, "We have not heard, neither have we known." But do you also, if you please, give reverential attention to the prophetic Scriptures, and they will make your way plainer for escaping the eternal punishments, and obtaining the eternal prizes of God. For He who gave the mouth for speech, and formed the ear to hear, and made the eye to see, will examine all things, and will judge righteous judgment, rendering merited awards to each. To those who by patient continuance in well-doing seek immortality, He will give life everlasting, joy, peace, rest, and abundance of good things, which neither hath eye seen, nor ear heard, nor hath it entered into the heart of man to conceive. But to the unbelieving and despisers, who obey not the truth, but are obedient to unrighteousness, when they shall have been filled with adulteries and fornications, and filthiness, and covetousness, and unlawful idolatries, there shall be anger and wrath, tribulation and anguish, and at the last everlasting fire shall possess such men. Since you said, "Show me thy God," this is my God, and I counsel you to fear Him and to trust Him.

Book II.

CHAPTER I.—OCCASION OF WRITING THIS BOOK.

When we had formerly some conversation, my very good friend Autolycus, and when you inquired who was my God, and for a little paid attention to my discourse, I made some explanations to you concerning my religion; and then having bid one another adieu, we went with much mutual friendliness each to his own house, although at first you had borne somewhat hard upon me. For you know and remember that you supposed our doctrine was foolishness. As you then afterwards urged me to do, I am desirous, though not educated to the art of speaking, of more accurately demonstrating, by means of this tractate, the vain labor and empty worship in which you are held; and I wish also, from a few of your own histories which you read, and perhaps do not yet quite understand, to make the truth plain to you.

CHAPTER II.—THE GODS ARE DESPISED WHEN THEY ARE MADE; BUT BECOME VALUABLE WHEN BOUGHT.

And in truth it does seem to me absurd that statuaries and carvers, or painters, or moulders, should both design and paint, and carve, and mould, and prepare gods, who, when they are produced by the artificers, are reckoned of no value; but as soon as they are purchased by some and placed in some so-called temple, or in some house, not only do those who bought them sacrifice to them, but also those who made and sold them come with much devotion, and apparatus of sacrifice, and libations, to worship them; and they reckon them gods, not seeing that they are just such as when they were made by themselves, whether stone, or brass, or wood, or color, or some other material. And this is your case, too, when you read the histories and genealogies of the so-called gods. For when you read of their births, you think of them as men, but afterwards you call them gods, and worship them, not reflecting nor understanding that, when born, they are exactly such beings as ye read of before.

CHAPTER III.—WHAT HAS BECOME OF THE GODS?

And of the gods of former times, if indeed they were begotten, the generation was sufficiently prolific. But now, where is their generation exhibited? For if of old they begot and were begotten, it is plain that even to the present time there should be gods begotten and born; or at least if it be not so, such a race will be reckoned impotent. For either they have waxed old, and on that account no longer beget, or they have died out and no longer exist. For if the gods were begotten, they ought to be born even until now, as men, too, are born; yea, much more numerous should the gods be than men, as the Sibyl says:—"For if the gods beget, and each remains
Immortal, then the race of gods must be more numerous than mortals, and the throng so great that mortals find no room to stand." For if the children begotten of men who are mortal and short-lived make an appearance even until now, and men have not ceased to be born, so that cities and villages are full, and even the country places also are inhabited, how ought not the gods, who, according to your poets, do not die, much rather to beget and be begotten, since you say that the gods were produced by generation? And why was the mount which is called Olympus formerly inhabited by the gods, but now lies deserted? Or why did Jupiter, in days of yore, dwell on Ida, and was known to dwell there, according to Homer and other poets, but now is beyond ken? And why was he found only in one part of the earth, and not everywhere? For either he neglected

the other parts, or was not able to be present everywhere and provide for all. For if he were, e.g., in an eastern place, he was not in the western; and if, on the other hand, he was present in the western parts, he was not in the eastern. But this is the attribute of God, the Highest and Almighty, and the living God, not only to be everywhere present, but also to see all things and to hear all, and by no means to be confined in a place; for if He were, then the place containing Him would be greater than He; for that which contains is greater than that which is contained. For God is not contained, but is Himself the place of all. But why has Jupiter left Ida? Was it because he died, or did that mountain no longer please him? And where has he gone? To heaven? No. But you will perhaps say, To Crete? Yes, for there, too, his tomb is shown to this day. Again, you will say, To Pisa, where he reflects glory on the hands of Phidias to this day. Let us, then, proceed to the writings of the philosophers and poets.

CHAPTER IV.—ABSURD OPINIONS OF THE PHILOSOPHERS CONCERNING GOD.

Some of the philosophers of the Porch say that there is no God at all; or, if there is, they say that He cares for none but Himself; and these views the folly of Epicurus and Chrysippus has set forth at large. And others say that all things are produced without external agency, and that the world is uncreated, and that nature is eternal; and have dared to give out that there is no providence of God at all, but maintain that God is only each man's conscience. And others again maintain that the spirit which pervades all things is God. But Plato and those of his school acknowledge indeed that God is uncreated, and the Father and Maker of all things; but then they maintain that matter as well as God is uncreated, and aver that it is coeval with God. But if God is uncreated and matter uncreated, God is no longer, according to the Platonists, the Creator of all things, nor, so far as their opinions hold, is the monarchy of God established. And further, as God, because He is uncreated, is also unalterable; so if matter, too, were uncreated, it also would be unalterable, and equal to God; for that which is created is mutable and alterable, but that which is uncreated is immutable and unalterable. And what great thing is it if God made the world out of existent materials? For even a human artist, when he gets material from some one, makes of it what he pleases.

But the power of God is manifested in this, that out of things that are not He makes whatever He pleases; just as the bestowal of life and motion is the prerogative of no other than God alone. For even man makes indeed an image, but reason and breath, or feeling, he cannot give to what he has made. But God has this property in excess of what man can do, in that He makes a work, endowed with reason, life, sensation. As, therefore, in all these respects God is more powerful than man, so also in this; that out of things that are not He creates and has created things that are, and whatever He pleases, as He pleases.

CHAPTER V.—OPINIONS OF HOMER AND HESIOD CONCERNING THE GODS.

So that the opinion of your philosophers and authors is discordant; for while the former has propounded the foregoing opinions, the poet Homer is found explaining the origin not only of the world, but also of the gods, on quite another hypothesis. For he says somewhere:
"Father of Gods, Oceanus, and she
Who bare the gods, their mother Tethys, too,
From whom all rivers spring, and every sea."
In saying which, however, he does not present God to us. For who does not know that the ocean is water? But if water, then not God. God indeed, if He is the creator of all things, as He certainly is, is the creator both of the water and of the seas. And Hesiod himself also declared the origin, not only of the gods, but also of the world itself. And though he said that the world was created, he showed no inclination to tell us by whom it was created. Besides, he said that Saturn, and his sons Jupiter, Neptune, and Pluto, were gods, though we find that

they are later born than the world. And he also relates how Saturn was assailed in war by his own son Jupiter; for he says:—

"His father Saturn he by might o'ercame,
And 'mong th' immortals ruled with justice wise,
And honors fit distributed to each."

Then he introduces in his poem the daughters of Jupiter, whom he names Muses, and as whose suppliant he appears, desiring to ascertain from them how all things were made; for he says:—

"Daughters of Jove, all hail! Grant me your aid
That I in numbers sweet and well-arrayed,
Of the immortal gods may sing the birth;
Who of the starry heav'ns were born, and earth;
Who, springing from the murky night at first,
Were by the briny ocean reared and nursed.
Tell, too, who form unto the earth first gave,
And rivers, and the boundless sea whose wave
Unwearied sinks, then rears its crest on high;
And how was spread yon glittering canopy
Of glistening stars that stud the wide-spread heaven.
Whence sprang the gods by whom all good is given?
Tell from their hands what varied gifts there came,
Riches to some, to others wealth, or fame;
How they have dwelt from the remotest time
In many-nooked Olympus' sunny clime.
These things, ye Muses, say, who ever dwell
Among Olympian shades—since ye can tell:
From the beginning there thy feet have strayed;
Then tell us which of all things first was made."

But how could the Muses, who are younger than the world, know these things? Or how could they relate to Hesiod [what was happening], when their father was not yet born?

Theophilus of Antioch

CHAPTER VI.—HESIOD ON THE ORIGIN OF THE WORLD.

And in a certain way he indeed admits matter [as self-existent] and the creation of the world [without a creator], saying:—
"First of all things was chaos made, and next
Broad-bosom'd earth's foundations firm were fixed,
Where safely the immortals dwell for aye,
Who in the snowy-peak'd Olympus stay.
Afterwards gloomy Tartarus had birth
In the recesses of broad-pathwayed earth,
And Love, ev'n among gods most beauteous still,
Who comes all-conquering, bending mind and will,
Delivering from care, and giving then
Wise counsel in the breasts of gods and men.
From chaos Erebus and night were born,
From night and Erebus sprung air and morn.
Earth in her likeness made the starry heaven,
That unto all things shelter might be given,
And that the blessed gods might there repose.
The lofty mountains by her power arose,
For the wood-nymphs she made the pleasant caves,
Begot the sterile sea with all his waves,
Loveless; but when by heaven her love was sought,
Then the deep-eddying ocean forth she brought."

And saying this, he has not yet explained by whom all this was made. For if chaos existed in the beginning, and matter of some sort, being uncreated, was previously existing, who was it that effected the change on its condition, and gave it a different order and shape? Did matter itself alter its own form and arrange itself into a world (for Jupiter was born, not only long after matter, but long after the world and many men; and so, too, was his father Saturn), or was there some ruling power which made it; I mean, of course, God, who also fashioned it into a world? Besides, he is found in every way to talk nonsense, and to contradict himself. For when he mentions earth, and sky, and sea, he gives us to understand that from these the gods were produced; and from these again [the gods] he declares that certain very dreadful men were sprung,—the race of the Titans and the Cyclopes, and a crowd of giants, and of the Egyptian gods,—or, rather, vain men, as Apollonides, surnamed Horapius, mentions in the book entitled *Semenouthi*, and in his other histories concerning the worship of the Egyptians and their kings, and the vain labors in which they engaged.

CHAPTER VII.—FABULOUS HEATHEN GENEALOGIES.

Why need I recount the Greek fables,—of Pluto, king of darkness, of Neptune descending beneath the sea, and embracing Melanippe and begetting a cannibal son,—or the many tales your writers have woven into their tragedies concerning the sons of Jupiter, and whose pedigree they register because they were born men, and not gods? And the comic poet Aristophanes, in the play called "The Birds," having taken upon him to handle the subject of the Creation, said that in the beginning the world was produced from an egg, saying:—

"A windy egg was laid by black-winged night
At first."

But Satyrus, also giving a history of the Alexandrine families, beginning from Philopator, who was also named Ptolemy, gives out that Bacchus was his progenitor; wherefore also Ptolemy was the founder of this family. Satyrus then speaks thus: That Dejanira was born of Bacchus and Althea, the daughter of Thestius; and from her and Hercules the son of Jupiter there sprang, as I suppose, Hyllus; and from him Cleodemus, and from him Aristomachus, and from him Temenus, and from him Ceisus, and from him Maron, and

from him Thestrus, and from him Acous, and from him Aristomidas, and from him Caranus, and from him Coenus, and from him Tyrimmas, and from him Perdiccas, and from him Philip, and from him Æropus, and from him Alcetas, and from him Amyntas, and from him Bocrus, and from him Meleager, and from him Arsinoë and from her and Lagus Ptolemy Soter, and from him and Arsinoe Ptolemy Euergetes, and from him and Berenicé, daughter of Maga, king of Cyrene, Ptolemy Philopator. Thus, then, stands the relationship of the Alexandrine kings to Bacchus. And therefore in the Dionysian tribe there are distinct families:
the Althean from Althea, who was the wife of Dionysus and daughter of Thestius; the family of Dejanira also, from her who was the daughter of Dionysus and Althea, and wife of Hercules;— whence, too, the families have their names: the family of Ariadne, from Ariadne, daughter of Minos and wife of Dionysus, a dutiful daughter, who had intercourse with Dionysus in another form; the Thestian, from Thestius, the father of Althea; the Thoantian, from Thoas, son of Dionysus; the Staphylian, from Staphylus, son of Dionysus; the Euænian, from Eunous, son of Dionysus; the Maronian, from Maron, son of Ariadne and Dionysus;— for all these are sons of Dionysus. And, indeed, many other names were thus originated, and exist to this day; as the Heraclidæ from Hercules, and the Apollonidæ from Apollo, and the Poseidonii from Poseidon, and from Zeus the Dii and Diogenæ.

CHAPTER VIII.— OPINIONS CONCERNING PROVIDENCE.

And why should I recount further the vast array of such names and genealogies? So that all the authors and poets, and those called philosophers, are wholly deceived; and so, too, are they who give heed to them. For they plentifully composed fables and foolish stories about their gods, and did not exhibit them as gods, but as men, and men, too, of whom some were drunken, and others fornicators and murderers. But also concerning the origin of the world, they uttered contradictory and absurd opinions. First, some of them, as we before explained, maintained that the world is uncreated. And those that said it was uncreated and self-producing contradicted those who propounded that it was created. For by conjecture and human conception they spoke, and not knowing the truth. And others, again, said that there was a providence, and destroyed the positions of the former writers. Aratus, indeed, says:—

> "From Jove begin my song; nor ever be
> The name unuttered: all are full of thee;
> The ways and haunts of men; the heavens and sea:
> On thee our being hangs; in thee we move;
> All are thy offspring and the seed of Jove.
> Benevolent, he warns mankind to good,
> Urges to toil and prompts the hope of food.
> He tells where cattle best may graze, and where
> The soil, deep-furrowed, yellow grain will bear.
> What time the husbandman should plant or sow,
> 'Tis his to tell, 'tis his alone to know."

Who, then, shall we believe: Aratus as here quoted, or Sophocles, when he says:—

> "And foresight of the future there is none;
> 'Tis best to live at random, as one can"?

And Homer, again, does not agree with this, for he says that virtue

> "Waxes or wanes in men as Jove decrees."

And Simonides says:—

> "No man nor state has virtue save from God;
> Counsel resides in God; and wretched man
> Has in himself nought but his wretchedness."

So, too, Euripides:—

"Apart from God, there's nothing owned by men."

And Menander:—

"Save God alone, there's none for us provides."

And Euripides again:—

"For when God wills to save, all things He'll bend
To serve as instruments to work His end."

And Thestius:—

"If God design to save you, safe you are,
Though sailing in mid-ocean on a mat."

And saying numberless things of a like kind, they contradicted themselves. At least Sophocles, who in another place denied Providence, says:—

"No mortal can evade the stroke of God."

Besides, they both introduced a multitude of gods, and yet spoke of a Unity; and against those who affirmed a Providence they maintained in opposition that there was no Providence. Wherefore Euripides says:—

"We labor much and spend our strength in vain,
For empty hope, not foresight, is our guide."

And without meaning to do so, they acknowledge that they know not the truth; but being inspired by demons and puffed up by them, they spoke at their instance whatever they said. For indeed the poets,—Homer, to wit, and Hesiod, being, as they say, inspired by the Muses,—spoke from a deceptive fancy, and not with a pure but an erring spirit. And this, indeed, clearly appears from the fact, that even to this day the possessed are sometimes exorcised in the name of the living and true God; and these spirits of error themselves confess that they are demons who also formerly inspired these writers. But sometimes some of them wakened up in soul, and, that they might be for a witness both to themselves and to all men, spoke things in harmony with the prophets regarding the monarchy of God, and the judgment and such like.

CHAPTER IX.—THE PROPHETS INSPIRED BY THE HOLY GHOST.

But men of God carrying in them a holy spirit and becoming prophets, being inspired and made wise by God, became God-taught, and holy, and righteous. Wherefore they were also deemed worthy of receiving this reward, that they should become instruments of God, and contain the wisdom that is from Him, through which wisdom they uttered both what regarded the creation of the world and all other things. For they predicted also pestilences, and famines, and wars. And there was not one or two, but many, at various times and seasons among the Hebrews; and also among the Greeks there was the Sibyl; and they all have spoken things consistent and harmonious with each other, both what happened before them and what happened in their own time, and what things are now being fulfilled in our own day: wherefore we are persuaded also concerning the future things that they will fall out, as also the first have been accomplished.

CHAPTER X.—THE WORLD CREATED BY GOD THROUGH THE WORD.

And first, they taught us with one consent that God made all things out of nothing; for nothing was coeval with God: but He being His own place, and wanting nothing, and existing before the ages, willed to make man by whom He might be known; for him, therefore, He prepared the world. For he that is created is also needy; but he that is uncreated stands in need of nothing. God, then, having His own Word internal within His own bowels, begat Him, emitting Him along with His own wisdom before all things. He had this Word as a helper in the things that were created by Him, and by Him He made all things. He is called "governing principle" [ἀρκή], because He rules, and is Lord of all things fashioned by Him. He, then, being Spirit of God, and governing principle, and wisdom, and power of the highest, came down upon the prophets, and through them spoke of the creation of the world and of all other things. For the prophets were not when the world came into existence, but the wisdom of God which was in Him, and His holy Word which was always present with Him. Wherefore He speaks thus by the prophet Solomon: "When He prepared the heavens I was there, and when He appointed the foundations of the earth I was by Him as one brought up with Him." And Moses, who lived many years before Solomon, or, rather, the Word of God by him as by an instrument, says, "In the beginning God created the heaven and the earth." First he named the "beginning," and "creation," then he thus introduced God; for not lightly and on slight occasion is it right to name God. For the divine wisdom foreknew that some would trifle and name a multitude of gods that do not exist. In order, therefore, that the living God might be known by His works, and that [it might be known that] by His Word God created the heavens and the earth, and all that is therein, he said, "In the beginning God created the heavens and the earth." Then having spoken of their creation, he explains to us: "And the earth was without form, and void, and darkness was upon the face of the deep; and the Spirit of God moved upon the water." This, sacred Scripture teaches at the outset, to show that matter, from which God made and fashioned the world, was in some manner created, being produced by God.

CHAPTER XI.—THE SIX DAYS' WORK DESCRIBED.

Now, the beginning of the creation is light; since light manifests the things that are created. Wherefore it is said: "And God said, Let light be, and light was; and God saw the light, that it was good," manifestly made good for man. "And God divided the light from the darkness; and God called the light Day, and the darkness He called Night. And the evening and the morning were the first day. And God said, Let there be a firmament in the midst of the waters, and let it divide the waters from the waters: and it was so. And God made the firmament, and divided the waters which were under the firmament from the waters which were above the firmament. And God called the firmament Heaven: and God saw that it was good. And the evening and the morning were the second day. And God said, let the water under the heaven be gathered into one place, and let the dry land appear: and it was so. And the waters were gathered together into their places, and the dry land appeared. And God called the dry land Earth, and the gathering together of the waters He called Seas: and God saw that it was good. And God said, Let the earth bring forth grass, the herb yielding seed after his kind and in his likeness, and the fruit-tree yielding fruit after his kind, whose seed is in itself, in his likeness: and it was so. And the earth brought forth grass, the herb yielding seed after his kind, and the fruit-tree yielding fruit, whose seed was in itself, after his kind, on the earth: and God saw that it was good. And the evening and the morning were the third day. And God said, Let there be lights in the firmament of the heaven, to give light on earth, to divide the day from the night; and let them be for signs, and for seasons, and for days, and for years; and let them be for lights in the firmament of the heaven, to give light upon the earth: and it was so. And God made two great lights; the greater light to rule the day, and the lesser light to rule the night: He made the stars also. And God set them in the firmament of the heaven to give light upon the earth, and to rule over the day and over the night, and to divide the light from the darkness: and God saw that it was good. And the evening and the morning were the fourth day. And God said, Let the waters bring forth the creeping things that have life, and fowl flying over the earth in the firmament of heaven: and it was so. And God created great whales, and every living creature that creepeth, which the waters brought forth after their kind, and every winged fowl after his kind: and God saw that it was good. And God blessed them, saying, Increase and multiply, and fill the waters of the sea, and let fowl multiply in the earth. And the evening and the morning were the fifth day. And God said, let the earth bring forth the living creature after his kind, cattle, and creeping thing, and beast of the earth after his kind: and it was so. And God made the beasts of the earth after their kind, and the cattle after their kind, and all the creeping things of the earth. And God said, Let us make man in our image, after our likeness; and let them have dominion over the fish of the sea, and over the fowl of the heaven, and over the cattle, and over all the earth, and over every creeping thing that creepeth upon the earth. And God created man: in the image of God created He him; male and female created He them. And God blessed them, saying, Be fruitful, and multiply, and replenish the earth, and subdue it, and have dominion over the fish of the sea, and over the fowl of the heaven, and over all cattle, and over all the earth, and over all the creeping things that creep upon the earth. And God said, Behold I have given you every herb bearing seed, which is upon the face of all the earth, and every tree in the which is the fruit of a tree yielding seed; to you it shall be for meat, and to all the beasts of the earth, and to all the fowls of heaven, and to every creeping thing that creepeth upon the earth, which has in it the breath of life; every green herb for meat: and it was so. And God saw everything that He had made, and, behold, it was very good. And the evening and the morning were the sixth day. And the heaven and the earth were finished, and all the host of them. And on the sixth day God finished His works which He made, and rested on the seventh day from all His works which He made. And God blessed the seventh day, and sanctified it; because in it He rested from all His works which God began to create."

CHAPTER XII.—THE GLORY OF THE SIX DAYS' WORK.

Of this six days' work no man can give a worthy explanation and description of all its parts, not though he had ten thousand tongues and ten thousand mouths; nay, though he were to live ten thousand years, sojourning in this life, not even so could he utter anything worthy of these things, on account of the exceeding greatness and riches of the wisdom of God which there is in the six days' work above narrated. Many writers indeed have imitated [the narration], and essayed to give an explanation of these things; yet, though they thence derived some suggestions, both concerning the creation of the world and the nature of man, they have emitted no slightest spark of truth. And the utterances of the philosophers, and writers, and poets have an appearance of trustworthiness, on account of the beauty of their diction; but their discourse is proved to be foolish and idle, because the multitude of their nonsensical frivolities is very great; and not a stray morsel of truth is found in them. For even if any truth seems to have been uttered by them, it has a mixture of error. And as a deleterious drug, when mixed with honey or wine, or some other thing, makes the whole [mixture] hurtful and profitless; so also eloquence is in their case found to be labor in vain; yea, rather an injurious thing to those who credit it. Moreover, [they spoke] concerning the seventh day, which all men acknowledge; but the most know not that what among the Hebrews is called the "Sabbath," is translated into Greek the "Seventh" (ἑβδομάς), a name which is adopted by every nation, although they know not the reason of the appellation. And as for what the poet Hesiod says of Erebus being produced from chaos, as well as the earth and love which lords it over *his* [Hesiod's] gods and men, his dictum is shown to be idle and frigid, and quite foreign to the truth. For it is not meet that God be conquered by pleasure; since even men of temperance abstain from all base pleasure and wicked lust.

CHAPTER XIII.—REMARKS ON THE CREATION OF THE WORLD.

Moreover, his [Hesiod's] human, and mean, and very weak conception, so far as regards God, is discovered in his beginning to relate the creation of all things from the earthly things here below. For man, being below, begins to build from the earth, and cannot in order make the roof, unless he has first laid the foundation. But the power of God is shown in this, that, first of all, He creates out of nothing, according to His will, the things that are made. "For the things which are impossible with men are possible with God." Wherefore, also, the prophet mentioned that the creation of the heavens first of all took place, as a kind of roof, saying: "At the first God created the heavens"—that is, that by means of the "first" principle the heavens were made, as we have already shown. And by "earth" he means the ground and foundation, as by "the deep" he means the multitude of waters; and "darkness" he speaks of, on account of the heaven which God made covering the waters and the earth like a lid. And by the Spirit which is borne above the waters, he means that which God gave for animating the creation, as he gave life to man, mixing what is fine with what is fine. For the Spirit is fine, and the water is fine, that the Spirit may nourish the water, and the water penetrating everywhere along with the Spirit, may nourish creation. For the Spirit being one, and holding the place of light, was between the water and the heaven, in order that the darkness might not in any way communicate with the heaven, which was nearer God, before God said, "Let there be light." The heaven, therefore, being like a dome-shaped covering, comprehended matter which was like a clod. And so another prophet, Isaiah by name, spoke in these words: "It is God who made the heavens as a vault, and stretched them as a tent to dwell in." The command, then, of God, that is, His Word, shining as a lamp in an enclosed chamber, lit up all that was under heaven, when He had made light apart from the world. And the light God called Day, and the darkness Night. Since man would not have been able to call the light Day, or the darkness Night, nor, indeed, to have given names to the other things, had not he received the nomenclature from God, who made the things themselves. In the very beginning, therefore, of the history and genesis of the world, the holy Scripture spoke not concerning this firmament [which we see], but concerning another heaven, which is to us invisible, after which this heaven which we see has been called "firmament," and to which half the water was taken up that it might serve for rains, and showers, and dews to mankind. And half the water was left on earth for rivers, and fountains, and seas. The water, then, covering all the earth, and specially its hollow places, God, through His Word, next caused the waters to be collected into one collection, and the dry land to become visible, which formerly had been invisible. The earth thus becoming visible, was yet without form. God therefore formed and adorned it with all kinds of herbs, and seeds and plants.

CHAPTER XIV.—THE WORLD COMPARED TO THE SEA.

Consider, further, their variety, and diverse beauty, and multitude, and how through them resurrection is exhibited, for a pattern of the resurrection of all men which is to be. For who that considers it will not marvel that a fig-tree is produced from a fig-seed, or that very huge trees grow from the other very little seeds? And we say that the world resembles the sea. For as the sea, if it had not had the influx and supply of the rivers and fountains to nourish it, would long since have been parched by reason of its saltness; so also the world, if it had not had the law of God and the prophets flowing and welling up sweetness, and compassion, and righteousness, and the doctrine of the holy commandments of God, would long ere now have come to ruin, by reason of the wickedness and sin which abound in it. And as in the sea there are islands, some of them habitable, and well-watered, and fruitful, with havens and harbors in which the storm-tossed may find refuge,—so God has given to the world which is driven and tempest-tossed by sins, assemblies—we mean holy churches—in which survive the doctrines of the truth, as in the island-harbors of good anchorage; and into these run those who desire to be saved, being lovers of the truth, and wishing to escape the wrath and judgment of God. And as, again, there are other islands, rocky and without water, and barren, and infested by wild beasts, and uninhabitable, and serving only to injure navigators and the storm-tossed, on which ships are wrecked, and those driven among them perish,—so there are doctrines of error—I mean heresies—which destroy those who approach them. For they are not guided by the word of truth; but as pirates, when they have filled their vessels, drive them on the fore-mentioned places, that they may spoil them: so also it happens in the case of those who err from the truth, that they are all totally ruined by their error.

CHAPTER XV.—OF THE FOURTH DAY.

On the fourth day the luminaries were made; because God, who possesses foreknowledge, knew the follies of the vain philosophers, that they were going to say, that the things which grow on the earth are produced from the heavenly bodies, so as to exclude God. In order, therefore, that the truth might be obvious, the plants and seeds were produced prior to the heavenly bodies, for what is posterior cannot produce that which is prior. And these contain the pattern and type of a great mystery. For the sun is a type of God, and the moon of man.
And as the sun far surpasses the moon in power and glory, so far does God surpass man. And as the sun remains ever full, never becoming less, so does God always abide perfect, being full of all power, and understanding, and wisdom, and immortality, and all good. But the moon wanes monthly, and in a manner dies, being a type of man; then it is born again, and is crescent, for a pattern of the future resurrection. In like manner also the three days which were before the luminaries, are types of the Trinity, of God, and His Word, and His wisdom. And the

fourth is the type of man, who needs light, that so there may be God, the Word, wisdom, man. Wherefore also on the fourth day the lights were made. The disposition of the stars, too, contains a type of the arrangement and order of the righteous and pious, and of those who keep the law and commandments of God. For the brilliant and bright stars are an imitation of the prophets, and therefore they remain fixed, not declining, nor passing from place to place. And those which hold the second place in brightness, are types of the people of the righteous. And those, again, which change their position, and flee from place to place, which also are called planets, they too are a type of the men who have wandered from God, abandoning His law and commandments.

CHAPTER XVI.—OF THE FIFTH DAY.

On the fifth day the living creatures which proceed from the waters were produced, through which also is revealed the manifold wisdom of God in these things; for who could count their multitude and very various kinds? Moreover, the things proceeding from the waters were blessed by God, that this also might be a sign of men's being destined to receive repentance and remission of sins, through the water and laver of regeneration,—as many as come to the truth, and are born again, and receive blessing from God. But the monsters of the deep and the birds of prey are a similitude of covetous men and transgressors. For as the fish and the fowls are of one nature,— some indeed abide in their natural state, and do no harm to those weaker than themselves, but keep the law of God, and eat of the seeds of the earth; others of them, again, transgress the law of God, and eat flesh, and injure those weaker than themselves: thus, too, the righteous, keeping the law of God, bite and injure none, but live holily and righteously. But robbers, and murderers, and godless persons are like monsters of the deep, and wild beasts, and birds of prey; for they virtually devour those weaker than themselves. The race, then, of fishes and of creeping things, though partaking of God's blessing, received no very distinguishing property.

CHAPTER XVII.—OF THE SIXTH DAY.

And on the sixth day, God having made the quadrupeds, and wild beasts, and the land reptiles, pronounced no blessing upon them, reserving His blessing for man, whom He was about to create on the sixth day. The quadrupeds, too, and wild beasts, were made for a type of some men, who neither know nor worship God, but mind earthly things, and repent not. For those who turn from their iniquities and live righteously, in spirit fly upwards like birds, and mind the things that are above, and are well-pleasing to the will of God. But those who do not know nor worship God, are like birds which have wings, but cannot fly nor soar to the high things of God. Thus, too, though such persons are called men, yet being pressed down with sins, they mind groveling and earthly things. And the animals are named wild beasts [θηρία], from their being hunted [θηρεύεσθαι], not as if they had been made evil or venomous from the first—for nothing was made evil by God, but all things good, yea, very good,—but the sin in which man was concerned brought evil upon them. For when man transgressed, they also transgressed with him. For as, if the master of the house himself acts rightly, the domestics also of necessity conduct themselves well; but if the master sins, the servants also sin with him; so in like manner it came to pass, that in the case of man's sin, he being master, all that was subject to him sinned with him. When, therefore, man again shall have made his way back to his natural condition, and no longer does evil, those also shall be restored to their original gentleness.

CHAPTER XVIII.—THE CREATION OF MAN.

But as to what relates to the creation of man, his own creation cannot be explained by man, though it is a succinct account of it which Holy Scripture gives. For when God said, "Let Us make man in Our image, after Our likeness," He first intimates the dignity of man. For God having made all things by His Word, and having reckoned them all mere byeworks, reckons the creation of man to be the only work worthy of His own hands. Moreover, God is found, as if needing help, to say, "Let Us make man in Our image, after Our likeness." But to no one else than to His own Word and wisdom did He say, "Let Us make." And when He had made and blessed him, that he might increase and replenish the earth, He put all things under his dominion, and at his service; and He appointed from the first that he should find nutriment from the fruits of the earth, and from seeds, and herbs, and acorns, having at the same time appointed that the animals be of habits similar to man's, that they also might eat of the seeds of the earth.

CHAPTER XIX.—MAN IS PLACED IN PARADISE.

God having thus completed the heavens, and the earth, and the sea, and all that are in them, on the sixth day, rested on the seventh day from all His works which He made. Then Holy Scripture gives a summary in these words: "This is the book of the generation of the heavens and the earth, when they were created, in the day that the Lord made the heavens and the earth, and every green thing of the field, before it was made, and every herb of the field before it grew. For God had not caused it to rain upon the earth, and there was not a man to till the ground." By this He signifies to us, that the whole earth was at that time watered by a divine fountain, and had no need that man should till it; but the earth produced all things spontaneously by the command of God, that man might not be wearied by tilling it. But that the creation of man might be made plain, so that there should not seem to be an insoluble problem existing among men, since God had said, "Let Us make man;" and since His creation was not yet plainly related, Scripture teaches us, saying: "And a fountain went up out of the earth, and watered the face of the whole earth; and God

Theophilus of Antioch

made man of the dust of the earth, and breathed into his face the breath of life, and man became a living soul." Whence also by most persons the soul is called immortal. And after the formation of man, God chose out for him a region among the places of the East, excellent for light, brilliant with a very bright atmosphere, [abundant] in the finest plants; and in this He placed man.

CHAPTER XX.—THE SCRIPTURAL ACCOUNT OF PARADISE.

Scripture thus relates the words of the sacred history: "And God planted Paradise, eastward, in Eden; and there He put the man whom He had formed. And out of the ground made God to grow every tree that is pleasant to the sight, and good for food; the tree of life also in the midst of Paradise, and the tree of the knowledge of good and evil. And a river flows out of Eden, to water the garden; thence it is parted into four heads. The name of the first is Pison: that is it which compasseth the whole land of Havilah, where there is gold; and the gold of that land is good, and there is bdellium and the onyx stone. And the name of the second river is Gihon: the same is it that compasseth the whole land of Ethiopia. And the third river is Tigris: this is it which goeth toward Syria. And the fourth river is Euphrates. And the Lord God took the man whom He had made, and put him in the garden, to till and to keep it. And God commanded Adam, saying, Of every tree that is in the garden thou mayest freely eat; but of the tree of the knowledge of good and evil, ye shall not eat of it; for in the day ye eat of it ye shall surely die. And the Lord God said, it is not good that the man should be alone; let Us make him a helpmeet for him. And out of the ground God formed all the beasts of the field, and all the fowls of heaven, and brought them to Adam. And whatsoever Adam called every living creature, that was the name thereof. And Adam gave names to all cattle, and to the fowls of the air, and to all the beasts of the field. But for Adam there was not found a helpmeet for him. And God caused an ecstasy to fall upon Adam, and he slept; and He took one of his ribs, and closed up the flesh instead thereof. And the rib, which the Lord God had taken from man, made He a woman, and brought her unto Adam. And Adam said, this is now bone of my bones, and flesh of my flesh; she shall be called Woman, because she was taken out of man. Therefore shall a man leave his father and his mother, and shall cleave unto his wife, and they two shall be one flesh. And they were both naked, Adam and his wife, and were not ashamed."

CHAPTER XXI.—OF THE FALL OF MAN.

"Now the serpent was more subtle than any beast of the field which the Lord God had made. And the serpent said to the woman, why hath God said, Ye shall not eat of every tree of the garden? And the woman said unto the serpent, we eat of every tree of the garden, but of the fruit of the tree which is in the midst of the garden God hath said, Ye shall not eat of it, neither shall ye touch it, lest ye die. And the serpent said unto the woman, ye shall not surely die. For God doth know that in the day ye eat thereof, then your eyes shall be opened, and ye shall be as gods, knowing good and evil. And the woman saw that the tree was good for food, and that it was pleasant to the eyes, and a tree to be desired to make one wise; and having taken of the fruit thereof, she did eat, and gave also unto her husband with her: and they did eat. And the eyes of them both were opened, and they knew that they were naked; and they sewed fig leaves together, and made themselves aprons. And they heard the voice of the Lord God walking in the garden in the cool of the day, and Adam and his wife hid themselves from the presence of the Lord God amongst the trees of the garden. And the Lord God called unto Adam, and said unto him, where art thou? And he said unto Him, I heard Thy voice in the garden, and I was afraid, because I was naked, and I hid myself. And He said unto him, Who told thee that thou wast naked, unless thou hast eaten of the tree whereof I commanded thee that thou shouldest not eat? And Adam said, the woman whom Thou gavest to be with me, she gave me of the tree, and

I did eat. And God said to the woman, what is this that thou hast done? And the woman said, the serpent beguiled me, and I did eat. And the Lord God said unto the serpent, Because thou hast done this, thou art accursed above all the beasts of the earth; on thy breast and belly shalt thou go, and dust shalt thou eat all the days of thy life: and I will put enmity between thee and the woman, and between thy seed and her seed; it shall bruise thy head, and thou shalt bruise his heel. And to the woman He said, I will greatly multiply thy sorrow and thy travail: in sorrow shalt thou bring forth children; and thy desire shall be to thy husband, and he shall rule over thee. And unto Adam He said, Because thou hast hearkened unto the voice of thy wife, and hast eaten of the tree of which I commanded thee, saying, Thou shalt not eat of it; cursed is the ground in thy works: in sorrow shalt thou eat of it all the days of thy life; thorns and thistles shall it bring forth to thee; and thou shalt eat the herb of the field. In the sweat of thy face shalt thou eat thy bread, till thou return unto the earth; for out of it wast thou taken: for dust thou art, and unto dust shalt thou return." Such is the account given by Holy Scripture of the history of man and of Paradise.

CHAPTER XXII.—WHY GOD IS SAID TO HAVE WALKED.

You will say, then, to me: "You said that God ought not to be contained in a place, and how do you now say that He walked in Paradise?" Hear what I say. The God and Father, indeed, of all cannot be contained, and is not found in a place, for there is no place of His rest; but His Word, through whom He made all things, being His power and His wisdom, assuming the person of the Father and Lord of all, went to the garden in the person of God, and conversed with Adam. For the divine writing itself teaches us that Adam said that he had heard the voice. But what else is this voice but the Word of God, who is also His Son? Not as the poets and writers of myths talk of the sons of gods begotten from intercourse [with women], but as truth expounds, the Word, that always exists, residing within the heart of God. For before anything came into being He had Him as a counselor, being His own mind and thought. But when God wished to make all that He determined on, He begot this Word, uttered, the first-born of all creation, not Himself being emptied of the Word [Reason], but having begotten Reason, and always conversing with His Reason. And hence the holy writings teach us, and all the spirit-bearing [inspired] men, one of whom, John, says, "In the beginning was the Word, and the Word was with God," showing that at first God was alone, and the Word in Him. Then he says, "The Word was God; all things came into existence through Him; and apart from Him not one thing came into existence." The Word, then, being God, and being naturally produced from God, whenever the Father of the universe wills, He sends Him to any place; and He, coming, is both heard and seen, being sent by Him, and is found in a place.

CHAPTER XXIII.—THE TRUTH OF THE ACCOUNT IN GENESIS.

Man, therefore, God made on the sixth day, and made known this creation after the seventh day, when also He made Paradise, that he might be in a better and distinctly superior place. And that this is true, the fact itself proves. For how can one miss seeing that the pains which women suffer in childbed, and the oblivion of their labors which they afterwards enjoy, are sent in order that the word of God may be fulfilled, and that the race of men may increase and multiply? And do we not see also the judgment of the serpent,—how hatefully he crawls on his belly and eats the dust,—that we may have this, too, for a proof of the things which were said aforetime?

CHAPTER XXIV.—THE BEAUTY OF PARADISE.

God, then, caused to spring out of the earth every tree that is beautiful in appearance, or good for food. For at first there were only those things which were produced on the third day,—plants, and seeds, and herbs; but the things which were

in Paradise were made of a superior loveliness and beauty, since in it the plants were said to have been planted by God.
As to the rest of the plants, indeed, the world contained plants like them; but the two trees,—the tree of life and the tree of knowledge,—the rest of the earth possessed not, but only Paradise. And that Paradise is earth, and is planted on the earth, the Scripture states, saying: "And the Lord God planted Paradise in Eden eastwards, and placed man there; and out of the ground made the Lord God to grow every tree that is pleasant to the sight and good for food." By the expressions, therefore, "out of the ground," and "eastwards," the holy writing clearly teaches us that Paradise is under this heaven, under which the east and the earth are. And the Hebrew word Eden signifies "delight." And it was signified that a river flowed out of Eden to water Paradise, and after that divides into four heads; of which the two called Pison and Gihon water the eastern parts, especially Gihon, which encompasses the whole land of Ethiopia, and which, they say, reappears in Egypt under the name of Nile. And the other two rivers are manifestly recognizable by us—those called Tigris and Euphrates—for these border on our own regions. And God having placed man in Paradise, as has been said, to till and keep it, commanded him to eat of all the trees,—manifestly of the tree of life also; but only of the tree of knowledge He commanded him not to taste. And God transferred him from the earth, out of which he had been produced, into Paradise, giving him means of advancement, in order that, maturing and becoming perfect, and being even declared a god, he might thus ascend into heaven in possession of immortality. For man had been made a middle nature, neither wholly mortal, nor altogether immortal, but capable of either; so also the place, Paradise, was made in respect of beauty intermediate between earth and heaven. And by the expression, "till it," no other kind of labor is implied than the observance of God's command, lest, disobeying, he should destroy himself, as indeed he did destroy himself, by sin.

CHAPTER XXV.—GOD WAS JUSTIFIED IN FORBIDDING MAN TO EAT OF THE TREE OF KNOWLEDGE.

The tree of knowledge itself was good, and its fruit was good. For it was not the tree, as some think, but the disobedience, which had death in it. For there was nothing else in the fruit than only knowledge; but knowledge is good when one uses it discreetly. But Adam, being yet an infant in age, was on this account as yet unable to receive knowledge worthily. For now, also, when a child is born it is not at once able to eat bread, but is nourished first with milk, and then, with the increment of years, it advances to solid food. Thus, too, would it have been with Adam; for not as one who grudged him, as some suppose, did God command him not to eat of knowledge. But He wished also to make proof of him, whether he was submissive to His commandment. And at the same time He wished man, infant as he was, to remain for some time longer simple and sincere. For this is holy, not only with God, but also with men, that in simplicity and guilelessness subjection be yielded to parents. But if it is right that children be subject to parents, how much more to the God and Father of all things? Besides, it is unseemly that children in infancy be wise beyond their years; for as in stature one increases in an orderly progress, so also in wisdom. But as when a law has commanded abstinence from anything, and some one has not obeyed, it is obviously not the law which causes punishment, but the disobedience and transgression;—for a father sometimes enjoins on his own child abstinence from certain things, and when he does not obey the paternal order, he is flogged and punished on account of the disobedience; and in this case the actions themselves are not the [cause of] stripes, but the disobedience procures punishment for him who disobeys;—so also for the first man, disobedience procured his expulsion from Paradise. Not, therefore, as if there were any evil in the tree of knowledge; but from his disobedience did man draw, as from a fountain, labor, pain, grief, and at last fall a prey to death.

CHAPTER XXVI.—GOD'S GOODNESS IN EXPELLING MAN FROM PARADISE.

And God showed great kindness to man in this, that He did not suffer him to remain in sin for ever; but, as it were, by a kind of banishment, cast him out of Paradise, in order that, having by punishment expiated, within an appointed time, the sin, and having been disciplined, he should afterwards be restored. Wherefore also, when man had been formed in this world, it is mystically written in Genesis, as if he had been twice placed in Paradise; so that the one was fulfilled when he was placed there, and the second will be fulfilled after the resurrection and judgment. For just as a vessel, when on being fashioned it has some flaw, is remolded or remade, that it may become new and entire; so also it happens to man by death. For somehow or other he is broken up, that he may rise in the resurrection whole; I mean spotless, and righteous, and immortal. And as to God's calling, and saying, Where art thou, Adam? God did this, not as if ignorant of this; but, being long-suffering, He gave him an opportunity of repentance and confession.

CHAPTER XXVII.—THE NATURE OF MAN.

But some one will say to us, was man made by nature mortal? Certainly not. Was he, then, immortal? Neither do we affirm this. But one will say, was he, then, nothing? Not even this hits the mark. He was by nature neither mortal nor immortal. For if He had made him immortal from the beginning, He would have made him God. Again, if He had made him mortal, God would seem to be the cause of his death. Neither, then, immortal nor yet mortal did He make him, but, as we have said above, capable of both; so that if he should incline to the things of immortality, keeping the commandment of God, he should receive as reward from Him immortality, and should become God; but if, on the other hand, he should turn to the things of death, disobeying God, he should himself be the cause of death to himself. For God made man free, and with power over himself. That, then, which man brought upon himself through carelessness and disobedience, this God now vouchsafes to him as a gift through His own philanthropy and pity, when men obey Him. For as man, disobeying, drew death upon himself; so, obeying the will of God, he who desires is able to procure for himself life everlasting. For God has given us a law and holy commandments; and every one who keeps these can be saved, and, obtaining the resurrection, can inherit incorruption.

CHAPTER XXVIII.—WHY EVE WAS FORMED OF ADAM'S RIB.

And Adam having been cast out of Paradise, in this condition knew Eve his wife, whom God had formed into a wife for him out of his rib. And this He did, not as if He were unable to make his wife separately, but God foreknew that man would call upon a number of gods. And having this prescience, and knowing that through the serpent error would introduce a number of gods which had no existence,—for there being but one God, even then error was striving to disseminate a multitude of gods, saying, "Ye shall be as gods;"—lest, then, it should be supposed that one God made the man and another the woman, therefore He made them both; and God made the woman together with the man, not only that thus the mystery of God's sole government might be exhibited, but also that their mutual affection might be greater. Therefore said Adam to Eve, "This is now bone of my bones, and flesh of my flesh." And besides, he prophesied, saying, "For this cause shall a man leave his father and his mother, and shall cleave unto his wife; and they two shall be one flesh;" which also itself has its fulfillment in ourselves. For who that marries lawfully does not despise mother and father, and his whole family connection, and all his household, cleaving to and becoming one with his own wife, fondly preferring her? So that often, for the sake of their wives, some submit even to death. This Eve, on account of her having been in the beginning deceived by the serpent, and become the author of sin, the wicked demon, who also is called Satan, who then spoke to her through the serpent, and who works even to this day in those men that are possessed by him, invokes as Eve. And he is called "demon" and "dragon," on account of his [ἀποδεδρακέναι] revolting from God. For at first he was an angel. And concerning his history there is a great deal to be said; wherefore I at present omit the relation of it, for I have also given an account of him in another place.

CHAPTER XXIX.—CAIN'S CRIME.

When, then, Adam knew Eve his wife, she conceived and bare a son, whose name was Cain; and she said, "I have gotten a man from God." And yet again she bare a second son, whose name was Abel, "who began to be a keeper of sheep, but Cain tilled the ground." Their history receives a very full narration, yea, even a detailed explanation: wherefore the book itself, which is entitled "The Genesis of the World," can more accurately inform those who are anxious to learn their story. When, then, Satan saw Adam and his wife not only still living, but also begetting children—being carried away with spite because he had not succeeded in putting them to death,—when he saw that Abel was well-pleasing to God, he wrought upon the heart of his brother called Cain, and caused him to kill his brother Abel. And thus did death get a beginning in this world, to find its way into every race of man, even to this day. But God, being pitiful, and wishing to afford to Cain, as to Adam, an opportunity of repentance and confession, said, "Where is Abel thy brother?" But Cain answered God contumaciously, saying, "I know not; am I my brother's keeper?" God, being thus made angry with him, said, "What hast thou done? The voice of thy brother's blood crieth to me from the earth, which opened her mouth to receive thy brother's blood from thy hand. Groaning and trembling shalt thou be on the earth." From that time the earth, through fear, no longer receives human blood, no, nor the blood of any animal; by which it appears that it is not the cause [of death], but man, who transgressed.

CHAPTER XXX.—CAIN'S FAMILY AND THEIR INVENTIONS.

Cain also himself had a son, whose name was Enoch; and he built a city, which he called by the name of his son, Enoch. From that time was there made a beginning of the building of cities, and this before the flood; not as Homer falsely says:—

"Not yet had men a city built."

And to Enoch was born a son, by name Gaidad; who begat a son called Meel; and Meel begat Mathusala; and Mathusala, Lamech. And Lamech took unto him two wives, whose names were Adah and Zillah. At that time there was made a beginning of polygamy, and also of music. For Lamech had three sons: Jabal, Jubal, Tubal. And Jabal became a keeper of cattle, and dwelt in tents; but Jubal is he who made known the psaltery and the harp; and Tubal became a smith, a forger in brass and iron. So far the seed of Cain is registered; and for the rest, the seed of his line has sunk into oblivion, on account of his fratricide of his brother. And, in place of Abel, God granted to Eve to conceive and bear a son, who was called Seth; from whom the remainder of the human race proceeds until now. And to those who desire to be informed regarding all generations, it is easy to give explanations by means of the Holy Scriptures. For, as we have already mentioned, this subject, the order of the genealogy of man, has been partly handled by us in another discourse, in the first book of *The History*. And all these things the Holy Spirit teaches us, who speaks through Moses and the rest of the prophets, so that the writings which belong to us godly people are more ancient, yea, and are shown to be more truthful, than all writers and poets. But also, concerning music, some have fabled that Apollo was the inventor, and others say that Orpheus discovered the art of music from the sweet voices of the birds. Their story is shown to be empty and vain, for these inventors lived many years after the flood. And what relates to Noah, who is called by some Deucalion, has been explained by us in the book before mentioned, and which, if you wish it, you are at liberty to read.

CHAPTER XXXI.—THE HISTORY AFTER THE FLOOD.

After the flood was there again a beginning of cities and kings, in the following manner:—the first city was Babylon, and Erech, and Accad, and Calneh, in the land of Shinar. And their king was called Nebroth [Nimrod]. From these came Asshur, from whom also the Assyrians receive their name. And Nimrod built the cities Nineveh and Rehoboth, and Calah, and Resen, between Nineveh and Calah; and Nineveh became a very great city. And another son of Shem, the son of Noah, by name Mizraim, begat Ludim, and those called Anamim, and Lehabim, and Naphtuhim, and Pathrusim, and Casluhim, out of whom came Philistin. Of the three sons of Noah, however, and of their death and genealogy, we have given a compendious register in the above-mentioned book. But now we will mention the remaining facts both concerning cities and kings, and the things that happened when there was one speech and one language. Before the dividing of the languages these fore-mentioned cities existed. But when men were about to be dispersed, they took counsel of their own judgment, and not at the instigation of God, to build a city, a tower whose top might reach into heaven, that they might make a glorious name to themselves. Since, therefore, they had dared, contrary to the will of God, to attempt a grand work, God destroyed their city, and overthrew their tower. From that time He confounded the languages of men, giving to each a different dialect. And similarly did the Sibyl speak, when she declared that wrath would come on the world. She says:—

"When are fulfilled the threats of the great God,
With which He threatened men, when formerly
In the Assyrian land they built a tower,
And all were of one speech, and wished to rise

> Even till they climbed unto the starry heaven,
> Then the Immortal raised a mighty wind
> And laid upon them strong necessity;
> For when the wind threw down the mighty tower,
> Then rose among mankind fierce strife and hate.
> One speech was changed to many dialects,
> And earth was filled with divers tribes and kings."

And so on. These things, then, happened in the land of the Chaldæans. And in the land of Canaan there was a city, by name Haran. And in these days, Pharaoh, who by the Egyptians was also called Nechaoth, was first king of Egypt, and thus the kings followed in succession. And in the land of Shinar, among those called Chaldæans, the first king was Arioch, and next after him Ellasar, and after him Chedorlaomer, king of Elam, and after him Tidal, king of the nations called Assyrians. And there were five other cities in the territory of Ham, the son of Noah; the first called Sodom, then Gomorrah, Admah, Zeboiim, and Balah, which was also called Zoar. And the names of their kings are these: Bera, king of Sodom; Birsha, king of Gomorrah; Shinab, king of Admah; Shemeber, king of Zeboiim; Bela, king of Zoar, which is also called Kephalac. These served Chedorlaomer, the king of the Assyrians, for twelve years, and in the thirteenth year they revolted from Chedorlaomer; and thus it came to pass at that time that the four Assyrian kings waged war upon the five kings. This was the first commencement of making war on the earth; and they destroyed the giants Karnaim, and the strong nations that were with them in their city, and the Horites of the mountains called Seir, as far as the plain of Paran, which is by the wilderness. And at that time there was a righteous king called Melchisedek, in the city of Salem, which now is Jerusalem. This was the first priest of all priests of the Most High God; and from him the above-named city Hierosolyma was called Jerusalem. And from his time priests were found in all the earth. And after him reigned Abimelech in Gerar; and after him another Abimelech.

Then reigned Ephron, surnamed the Hittite. Such are the names of the kings that were in former times. And the rest of the kings of the Assyrians, during an interval of many years, have been passed over in silence unrecorded, all writers narrating the events of our recent days. There were these kings of Assyria: Tiglath-Pileser, and after him Shalmaneser, then Sennacherib; and Adrammelech the Ethiopian, who also reigned over Egypt, was his triarch;—though these things, in comparison with our books, are quite recent.

CHAPTER XXXII.—HOW THE HUMAN RACE WAS DISPERSED.

Hence, therefore, may the loves of learning and of antiquity understand the history, and see that those things are recent which are told by us apart from the holy prophets. For though at first there were few men in the land of Arabia and Chaldæa, yet, after their languages were divided, they gradually began to multiply and spread over all the earth; and some of them tended towards the east to dwell there, and others to the parts of the great continent, and others northwards, so as to extend as far as Britain, in the Arctic regions. And others went to the land of Canaan, which is called Judæa, and Phoenicia, and the region of Ethiopia, and Egypt, and Libya, and the country called torrid, and the parts stretching towards the west; and the rest went to places by the sea, and Pamphylia, and Asia, and Greece, and Macedonia, and, besides, to Italy, and the whole country called Gaul, and Spain, and Germany; so that now the whole world is thus filled with inhabitants. Since then the occupation of the world by men was at first in three divisions,—in the east, and south, and west: afterwards, the remaining parts of the earth were inhabited, when men became very numerous. And the writers, not knowing these things, are forward to maintain that the world is shaped like a sphere, and to compare it to a cube. But how can they say what is true regarding these things, when they do not know about the creation of the world and its population? Men gradually increasing in number and multiplying on the earth, as we have already said, the islands also of the sea and the rest of the countries were inhabited.

CHAPTER XXXIII.—PROFANE HISTORY GIVES NO ACCOUNT OF THESE MATTERS.

Who, then, of those called sages, and poets, and historians, could tell us truly of these things, themselves being much later born, and introducing a multitude of gods, who were born so many years after the cities, and are more modern than kings, and nations, and wars? For they should have made mention of all events, even those which happened before the flood; both of the creation of the world and the formation of man, and the whole succession of events. The Egyptian or Chaldæan prophets, and the other writers, should have been able accurately to tell, if at least they spoke by a divine and pure spirit, and spoke truth in all that was uttered by them; and they should have announced not only things past or present, but also those that were to come upon the world. And therefore it is proved that all others have been in error; and that we Christians alone have possessed the truth, inasmuch as we are taught by the Holy Spirit, who spoke in the holy prophets, and foretold all things.

CHAPTER XXXIV.—THE PROPHETS ENJOINED HOLINESS OF LIFE.

And, for the rest, would that in a kindly spirit you would investigate divine things—I mean the things that are spoken by the prophets—in order that, by comparing what is said by us with the utterances of the others, you may be able to discover the truth. We have shown from their own histories, which they have compiled, that the names of those who are called gods, are found to be the names of men who lived among them, as we have shown above. And to this day their images are daily fashioned, idols, "the works of men's hands." And these the mass of foolish men serve, whilst they reject the maker and fashioner of all things and the nourisher of all breath of life, giving credit to vain doctrines through the deceitfulness of the senseless tradition received from their fathers. But God at least, the Father and Creator of the universe, did not abandon mankind, but gave a law, and sent holy prophets to declare and teach the race of men, that each one of us might awake and understand that there is one God. And they also taught us to refrain from unlawful idolatry, and adultery, and murder, fornication, theft, avarice, false swearing, wrath, and every incontinence and uncleanness; and that whatever a man would not wish to be done to himself, he should not do to another; and thus he who acts righteously shall escape the eternal punishments, and be thought worthy of the eternal life from God.

CHAPTER XXXV.—PRECEPTS FROM THE PROPHETIC BOOKS.

The divine law, then, not only forbids the worshipping of idols, but also of the heavenly bodies, the sun, the moon, or the other stars; yea, not heaven, nor earth, nor the sea, nor fountains, nor rivers, must be worshipped, but we must serve in holiness of heart and sincerity of purpose only the living and true God, who also is Maker of the universe. Wherefore saith the holy law: "Thou shalt not commit adultery; thou shalt not steal; thou shalt not bear false witness; thou shalt not desire thy neighbor's wife." So also the prophets. Solomon indeed teaches us that we must not sin with so much as a turn of the eye, saying, "Let thine eyes look right on, and let thy eyelids look straight before thee." And Moses, who himself also was a prophet, says, concerning the sole government of God: "Your God is He who establishes the heaven, and forms the earth, whose hands have brought forth all the host of heaven; and He has not set these things before you that you should go after them." And Isaiah himself also says: "Thus saith the Lord God who established the heavens, and founded the earth and all that is therein, and giveth breath unto the people upon it, and spirit to them that walk therein. This is the Lord your God." And again, through him He says: "I have made the earth, and man upon it. I by my hand have established the heavens." And in

another chapter, "This is your God, who created the ends of the earth; He hungereth not, neither is weary, and there is no searching of His understanding." So, too, Jeremiah says:
"Who hath made the earth by His power, and established the world by His wisdom, and by His discretion hath stretched out the heavens, and a mass of water in the heavens, and He caused the clouds to ascend from the ends of the earth; He made lightnings with rain, and brought forth winds out of His treasures." One can see how consistently and harmoniously all the prophets spoke, having given utterance through one and the same spirit concerning the unity of God, and the creation of the world, and the formation of man. Moreover, they were in sore travail, bewailing the godless race of men, and they reproached those, who seemed to be wise, for their error and hardness of heart. Jeremiah, indeed, said: "Every man is brutishly gone astray from the knowledge of Him; every founder is confounded by his graven images; in vain the silversmith makes his molten images; there is no breath in them: in the day of their visitation they shall perish." The same, too, says David: "They are corrupt, they have done abominable works; there is none that doeth good, no, not one; they have all gone aside, they have together become profitless." So also Habakkuk: "What profiteth the graven image that he has graven it a lying image? Woe to him that saith to the stone, Awake; and to the wood, Arise." Likewise spoke the other prophets of the truth.

And why should I recount the multitude of prophets, who are numerous, and said ten thousand things consistently and harmoniously? For those who desire it, can, by reading what they uttered, accurately understand the truth, and no longer be carried away by opinion and profitless labor. These, then, whom we have already mentioned, were prophets among the Hebrews,—illiterate, and shepherds, and uneducated.

CHAPTER XXXVI.—PROPHECIES OF THE SIBYL.

And the Sibyl, who was a prophetess among the Greeks and the other nations, in the beginning of her prophecy, reproaches the race of men, saying:—

"How are ye still so quickly lifted up,
And how so thoughtless of the end of life,
Ye mortal men of flesh, who are but naught?
Do ye not tremble, nor fear God most high?
Your Overseer, the Knower, Seer of all,
Who ever keeps those whom His hand first made,
Puts His sweet Spirit into all His works,
And gives Him for a guide to mortal men.
There is one only uncreated God,
Who reigns alone, all-powerful, very great,
From whom is nothing hid. He sees all things,
Himself unseen by any mortal eye.
Can mortal man see the immortal God,
Or fleshly eyes, which shun the noontide beams,
Look upon Him, who dwells beyond the heavens?
Worship Him then, the self-existent God,
The unbegotten Ruler of the world,
Who only was from everlasting time,
And shall to everlasting still abide.
Of evil counsels ye shall reap the fruit,
Because ye have not honored the true God,
Nor offered to Him sacred hecatombs.
To those who dwell in Hades ye make gifts,
And unto demons offer sacrifice.
In madness and in pride ye have your walk;
And leaving the right way, ye wander wide,
And lose yourselves in pitfalls and in thorns.
Why do ye wander thus, O foolish men?
Cease your vain wanderings in the black, dark night;
Why follow darkness and perpetual gloom
When, see, there shines for you the blessed light?

Lo, He is clear—in Him there is no spot.
Turn, then, from darkness, and behold the day;
Be wise, and treasure wisdom in your breasts.
There is one God who sends the winds and rains,
The earthquakes, and the lightnings, and the plagues,
The famines, and the snow-storms, and the ice,
And all the woes that visit our sad race.
Nor these alone, but all things else He gives,
Ruling omnipotent in heaven and earth,
And self-existent from eternity."

And regarding those [gods] that are said to have been born, she said:—

"If all things that are born must also die,
"God cannot be produced by mortal man.
But there is only One, the All-Supreme,
Who made the heavens, with all their starry host,
The sun and moon; likewise the fruitful earth,
With all the waves of ocean, and the hills,
The fountains, and the ever flowing streams;
He also made the countless multitude
Of ocean creatures, and He keeps alive
All creeping things, both of the earth and sea;
And all the tuneful choir of birds He made,
Which cleave the air with wings, and with shrill pipe
Trill forth at morn their tender, clear-voiced song.
Within the deep glades of the hills He placed
A savage race of beasts; and unto men
He made all cattle subject, making man
The God-formed image, ruler over all,
And putting in subjection to his sway
Things many and incomprehensible.
For who of mortals can know all these things?
He only knows who made them at the first,
He the Creator, incorruptible,

Who dwells in upper air eternally;
Who proffers to the good most rich rewards,
And against evil and unrighteous men
Rouses revenge, and wrath, and bloody wars,
And pestilence, and many a tearful grief.
O man exalted vainly—say why thus
Hast thou so utterly destroyed thyself?
Have ye no shame worshipping beasts for gods?
And to believe the gods should steal your beasts,
Or that they need your vessels—is it not
Frenzy's most profitless and foolish thought?
Instead of dwelling in the golden heavens,
Ye see your gods become the prey of worms,
And hosts of creatures noisome and unclean.
O fools! ye worship serpents, dogs, and cats,
Birds, and the creeping things of earth and sea,
Images made with hands, statues of stone,
And heaps of rubbish by the wayside placed.
All these, and many more vain things, ye serve,
Worshipping things disgraceful even to name:
These are the gods who lead vain men astray,
From whose mouth streams of deadly poison flow.
But unto Him in whom alone is life,
Life, and undying, everlasting light;
Who pours into man's cup of life a joy
Sweeter than sweetest honey to his taste,—
Unto Him bow the head, to Him alone,
And walk in ways of everlasting peace.
Forsaking Him, ye all have turned aside,
And, in your raving folly, drained the cup
Of justice quite unmixed, pure, mastering, strong;
And ye will not again be sober men,
Ye will not come unto a sober mind,
And know your God and King, who looks on all:
Therefore, upon you burning fire shall come,
And ever ye shall daily burn in flames,

> Ashamed for ever of your useless gods.
> But those who worship the eternal God,
> They shall inherit everlasting life,
> Inhabiting the blooming realms of bliss,
> And feasting on sweet food from starry heaven."

That these things are true, and useful, and just, and profitable to all men, is obvious. Even the poets have spoken of the punishments of the wicked.

CHAPTER XXXVII.—THE TESTIMONIES OF THE POETS.

And that evil-doers must necessarily be punished in proportion to their deeds, has already been, as it were, oracularly uttered by some of the poets, as a witness both against themselves and against the wicked, declaring that they shall be punished. Æschylus said:—

"He who has done must also suffer."

And Pindar himself said:—

"It is fit that suffering follow doing."

So, too, Euripides:—

> "The deed rejoiced you—suffering endure;
> The taken enemy must needs be pain'd."

And again:—

"The foe's pain is the hero's meed."

And, similarly, Archilochus:—

> "One thing I know, I hold it ever true,
> The evil-doer evil shall endure."

Theophilus of Antioch

And that God sees all, and that nothing escapes His notice, but that, being long-suffering, He refrains until the time when He is to judge—concerning this, too, Dionysius said:—

> "The eye of Justice seeing all,
> Yet seemeth not to see."

And that God's judgment is to be, and that evils will suddenly overtake the wicked,—this, too, Æschylus declared, saying:—

> "Swift-footed is the approach of fate,
> And none can justice violate,
> But feels its stern hand soon or late.
> "'Tis with you, though unheard, unseen;
> You draw night's curtain in between,
> But even sleep affords no screen.
> "'Tis with you if you sleep or wake;
> And if abroad your way you take,
> Its still, stern watch you cannot break.
> "'Twill follow you, or cross your path;
> And even night no virtue hath
> To hide you from th' Avenger's wrath.
> "To show the ill the darkness flees;
> Then, if sin offers joy or ease,
> Oh stop, and think that some one sees!"

And may we not cite Simonides also?—

> "To men no evil comes unheralded;
> But God with sudden hand transforms all things."

Euripides again:—

> "The wicked and proud man's prosperity
> Is based on sand: his race abideth not;
> And time proclaims the wickedness of men."

Once more Euripides:—

"Not without judgment is the Deity,
But sees when oaths are struck unrighteously,
And when from men unwilling they are wrung."

And Sophocles:—

"If ills you do, ills also you must bear."

That God will make inquiry both concerning false swearing and concerning every other wickedness, they themselves have well-nigh predicted. And concerning the conflagration of the world, they have, willingly or unwillingly, spoken in conformity with the prophets, though they were much more recent, and stole these things from the law and the prophets. The poets corroborate the testimony of the prophets.

CHAPTER XXXVIII.—THE TEACHINGS OF THE GREEK POETS AND PHILOSOPHERS CONFIRMATORY OF THOSE OF THE HEBREW PROPHETS.

But what matters it whether they were before or after them? Certainly they did at all events utter things confirmatory of the prophets. Concerning the burning up of the world, Malachi the prophet foretold: "The day of the Lord cometh as a burning oven, and shall consume all the wicked." And Isaiah: "For the wrath of God is as a violent hail-storm, and as a rushing mountain torrent." The Sibyl, then, and the other prophets, yea, and the poets and philosophers, have clearly taught both concerning righteousness, and judgment, and punishment; and also concerning providence, that God cares for us, not only for the living among us, but also for those that are dead: though, indeed, they said this unwillingly, for they were convinced by the truth. And among the prophets indeed, Solomon said of the dead, "There shall be healing to thy flesh, and care taken of thy bones." And the same says David, "The bones which Thou hast broken shall rejoice." And in agreement with these sayings was that of Timocles:—

"The dead are pitied by the loving God."

And the writers who spoke of a multiplicity of gods came at length to the doctrine of the unity of God, and those who asserted chance spoke also of providence; and the advocates of impunity confessed there would be a judgment, and those who denied that there is a sensation after death acknowledged that there is. Homer, accordingly, though he had said,—

"Like fleeting vision passed the soul away,"

says in another place:—

"To Hades went the disembodied soul;"

And again:—

"That I may quickly pass through Hades' gates,
Me bury."

And as regards the others whom you have read, I think you know with sufficient accuracy how they have expressed themselves. But all these things will every one understand who seeks the wisdom of God, and is well pleasing to Him through faith and righteousness and the doing of good works. For one of the prophets whom we already mentioned, Hosea by name, said, "Who is wise, and he shall understand these things? prudent, and he shall know them? for the ways of the Lord are right, and the just shall walk in them: but the transgressors shall fall therein." He, then, who is desirous of learning, should learn much. Endeavour therefore to meet [with me] more frequently, that, by hearing the living voice, you may accurately ascertain the truth.

Book III.

CHAPTER I.—AUTOLYCUS NOT YET CONVINCED.

Theophilus to Autolycus, greeting: Seeing that writers are fond of composing a multitude of books for vainglory,—some concerning gods, and wars, and chronology, and some, too, concerning useless legends, and other such labor in vain, in which you also have been used to employ yourself until now, and do not grudge to endure that toil; but though you conversed with me, are still of opinion that the word of truth is an idle tale, and suppose that our writings are recent and modern;—on this account I also will not grudge the labor of
compendiously setting forth to you, God helping me, the antiquity of our books, reminding you of it in few words, that you may not grudge the labor of reading it, but may recognize the folly of the other authors.

CHAPTER II.—PROFANE AUTHORS HAD NO MEANS OF KNOWING THE TRUTH.

For it was fit that they who wrote should themselves have been eye-witnesses of those things concerning which they made assertions, or should accurately have ascertained them from those who had seen them; for they who write of things unascertained beat the air. For what did it profit Homer to have composed the Trojan war, and to have deceived many; or
Hesiod, the register of the theogony of those whom he calls gods; or Orpheus, the three hundred and sixty-five gods, whom in the end of his life he rejects, maintaining in his precepts that there is one God? What profit did the sphærography of the world's circle confer on Aratus, or those who held the same doctrine as he, except glory among men? And not even that did they reap as they deserved. And what truth did they utter? Or what good did their tragedies do to Euripides and Sophocles, or the other tragedians? Or their comedies to Menander and Aristophanes, and the other comedians? Or their histories to

Herodotus and Thucydides? Or the shrines and the pillars of Hercules to Pythagoras, or the Cynic philosophy to Diogenes? What good did it do Epicurus to maintain that there is no providence; or Empedocles to teach atheism; or Socrates to swear by the dog, and the goose, and the plane-tree, and Æsculapius struck by lightning, and the demons whom he invoked? And why did he willingly die? What reward, or of what kind, did he expect to receive after death? What did Plato's system of culture profit him? Or what benefit did the *rest* of the philosophers derive from their doctrines, not to enumerate the whole of them, since they are numerous? But these things we say, for the purpose of exhibiting their useless and godless opinions.

CHAPTER III.—THEIR CONTRADICTIONS.

For all these, having fallen in love with vain and empty reputation, neither themselves knew the truth, nor guided others to the truth: for the things which they said themselves convict them of speaking inconsistently; and most of them demolished their own doctrines. For not only did they refute one another, but some, too, even stultified their own teachings; so that their reputation has issued in shame and folly, for they are condemned by men of understanding. For either they made assertions concerning the gods, and afterwards taught that there was no god; or if they spoke even of the creation of the world, they finally said that all things were produced spontaneously. Yea, and even speaking of providence, they taught again that the world was not ruled by providence. But what? Did they not, when they essayed to write even of honorable conduct, teach the perpetration of lasciviousness, and fornication, and adultery; and did they not introduce hateful and unutterable wickedness? And they proclaim that their gods took the lead in committing unutterable acts of adultery, and in monstrous banquets. For who does not sing Saturn devouring his own children, and Jove his son gulping down Metis, and preparing for the gods a horrible feast, at which also they say that Vulcan, a lame blacksmith, did the waiting; and how Jove not only married Juno, his own sister, but also with foul mouth did abominable wickedness? And the rest of his deeds, as many as the poets sing, it is likely you are acquainted with. Why need I further recount the deeds of Neptune and Apollo, or Bacchus and Hercules, of the bosom-loving Minerva, and the shameless Venus, since in another place we have given a more accurate account of these?

CHAPTER IV.—HOW AUTOLYCUS HAD BEEN MISLED BY FALSE ACCUSATIONS AGAINST THE CHRISTIANS.

Nor indeed was there any necessity for my refuting these, except that I see you still in dubiety about the word of the truth. For though yourself prudent, you endure fools gladly. Otherwise you would not have been moved by senseless men to yield yourself to empty words, and to give credit to the prevalent rumor wherewith godless lips falsely accuse us, who are worshippers of God, and are called Christians, alleging that the wives of us all are held in common and made promiscuous use of; and that we even commit incest with our own sisters, and, what is most impious and barbarous of all, that we eat human flesh. But further, they say that our doctrine has but recently come to light, and that we have nothing to allege in proof of what we receive as truth, nor of our teaching, but that our doctrine is foolishness. I wonder, then, chiefly that you, who in other matters are studious, and a scrutinizer of all things, give but a careless hearing to us. For, if it were possible for you, you would not grudge to spend the night in the libraries.

CHAPTER V.—PHILOSOPHERS INCULCATE CANNIBALISM.

Since, then, you have read much, what is your opinion of the precepts of Zeno, and Diogenes, and Cleanthes, which their books contain, inculcating the eating of human flesh: that fathers be cooked and eaten by their own children; and that if any one refuse or reject a part of this infamous food, he himself be devoured who will riot eat? An utterance even more godless than these is found,—that, namely, of Diogenes, who teaches children to bring their own parents in sacrifice, and devour them. And does not the historian Herodotus narrate that Cambyses, when he had slaughtered the children of Harpagus, cooked them also, and set them as a meal before their father? And, still further, he narrates that among the Indians the parents are eaten by their own children. Oh! the godless teaching of those who recorded, yea, rather, inculcated such things! Oh! their wickedness and godlessness! Oh! the conception of those who thus accurately philosophized, and profess philosophy! For they who taught these doctrines have filled the world with iniquity.

CHAPTER VI.—OTHER OPINIONS OF THE PHILOSOPHERS.

And regarding lawless conduct, those who have blindly wandered into the choir of philosophy have, almost to a man, spoken with one voice. Certainly Plato, to mention him first who seems to have been the most respectable philosopher among them, expressly, as it were, legislates in his first book, entitled *The Republic*, that the wives of all be common, using the precedent of the son of Jupiter and the lawgiver of the Cretans, in order that under this pretext there might be an abundant offspring from the best persons, and that those who were worn with toil might be comforted by such intercourse. And Epicurus himself, too, as well as teaching atheism, teaches along with it incest with mothers and sisters, and this in transgression of the laws which forbid it; for Solon distinctly legislated regarding this, in order that from a married parent children might lawfully spring, that they might not be born of adultery, so that no one should honor as his father him who was not his father, or dishonor him who was really his father, through ignorance that he was so. And these things the other laws of the Romans and Greeks also prohibit. Why, then, do Epicurus and the Stoics teach incest and sodomy, with which doctrines they have filled libraries, so that from boyhood this lawless intercourse is learned? And why should I further spend time on them, since even of those they call gods they relate similar things?

CHAPTER VII.—VARYING DOCTRINE CONCERNING THE GODS.

For after they had said that these are gods, they again made them of no account. For some said that they were composed of atoms; and others, again, that they eventuate in atoms; and they say that the gods have no more power than men. Plato, too, though he says these are gods, would have them composed of matter. And Pythagoras, after he had made such a toil and moil about the gods, and travelled up and down [for information], at last determines that all things are produced naturally and spontaneously, and that the gods care nothing for men. And how many atheistic opinions Clitomachus the academician introduced, [I need not recount.] And did not Critias and Protagoras of Abdera say, "For whether the gods exist, I am not able to affirm concerning them, nor to explain of what nature they are; for there are many things would prevent me"? And to speak of the opinions of the most atheistical,
Euhemerus, is superfluous. For having made many daring assertions concerning the gods, he at last would absolutely deny their existence, and have all things to be governed by self-regulated action. And Plato, who spoke so much of the unity of God and of the soul of man, asserting that the soul is immortal, is not he himself afterwards found, inconsistently with himself, to maintain that some souls pass into other men, and that others take their departure into irrational animals? How can his doctrine fail to seem dreadful and monstrous—to those at least who have any judgment—that he who was once a man shall afterwards be a wolf, or a dog, or an ass, or some other irrational brute? Pythagoras, too, is found venting similar nonsense, besides his demolishing providence. Which of them, then, shall we believe? Philemon, the comic poet, who says,—

"Good hope have they who praise and serve the gods;"

or those whom we have mentioned—Euhemerus, and Epicurus, and Pythagoras, and the others who deny that the gods are to be worshipped, and who abolish providence? Concerning God and providence, Ariston said:—

> "Be of good courage: God will still preserve
> And greatly help all those who so deserve.
> If no promotion waits on faithful men,
> Say what advantage goodness offers then.
> 'Tis granted—yet I often see the just
> Faring but ill, from ev'ry honor thrust;
> While they whose own advancement is their aim,
> Oft in this present life have all they claim.
> But we must look beyond, and wait the end,
> That consummation to which all things tend.
> 'Tis not, as vain and wicked men have said,
> By an unbridled destiny we're led:
> It is not blinded chance that rules the world,
> Nor uncontrolled are all things onward hurled.
> The wicked blinds himself with this belief;
> But be ye sure, of all rewards, the chief
> Is still reserved for those who holy live;
> And Providence to wicked men will give
> Only the just reward which is their meed,
> And fitting punishment for each bad deed."

And one can see how inconsistent with each other are the things which others, and indeed almost the majority, have said about God and providence. For some have absolutely cancelled God and providence; and others, again, have affirmed God, and have avowed that all things are governed by providence. The intelligent hearer and reader must therefore give minute attention to their expressions; as also Simylus said: "It is the custom of the poets to name by a common designation the surpassingly wicked and the excellent; we therefore must discriminate." As also Philemon says: "A senseless man who sits and merely hears is a troublesome feature; for he does not blame himself, so foolish is he." We must then give attention, and consider what is said, critically inquiring into what has been uttered by the philosophers and the poets.

CHAPTER VIII.—WICKEDNESS ATTRIBUTED TO THE GODS BY HEATHEN WRITERS.

For, denying that there are gods, they again acknowledge their existence, and they said they committed grossly wicked deeds. And, first, of Jove the poets euphoniously sing the wicked actions. And Chrysippus, who talked a deal of nonsense, is he not found publishing that Juno had the foulest intercourse with Jupiter? For why should I recount the impurities of the so-called mother of the gods, or of Jupiter Latiaris thirsting for human blood, or the castrated Attis; or of Jupiter, surnamed Tragedian, and how he defiled himself, as they say, and now is worshipped among the Romans as a god? I am silent about the temples of Antinous, and of the others whom you call gods. For when related to sensible persons, they excite laughter. They who elaborated such a philosophy regarding either the non-existence of God, or promiscuous intercourse and beastly concubinage, are themselves condemned by their own teachings. Moreover, we find from the writings they composed that the eating of human flesh was received among them; and they record that those whom they honor as gods were the first to do these things.

CHAPTER IX.—CHRISTIAN DOCTRINE OF GOD AND HIS LAW.

Now we also confess that God exists, but that He is one, the creator, and maker, and fashioner of this universe; and we know that all things are arranged by His providence, but by Him alone. And we have learned a holy law; but we have as

lawgiver Him who is really God, who teaches us to act righteously, and to be pious, and to do good. And concerning Piety He says, "Thou shalt have no other gods before me. Thou shalt not make unto thee any graven image, or any likeness of anything that is in heaven above, or that is in the earth beneath, or that is in the water under the earth: thou shalt not bow down thyself to them, nor serve them: for I am the Lord thy God." And of doing good He said: "Honor thy father and thy mother; that it may be well with thee, and that thy days may be long in the land which I the Lord God give thee." Again, concerning righteousness: "Thou shalt not commit adultery. Thou shalt not kill. Thou shalt not steal. Thou shalt not bear false witness against thy neighbor. Thou shalt not covet thy neighbor's wife, thou shalt not covet thy neighbor's house, nor his land, nor his man-servant, nor his maid-servant, nor his ox, nor his beast of burden, nor any of his cattle, nor anything that is thy neighbor's. Thou shalt not wrest the judgment of the poor in his cause. From every unjust matter keep thee far.
The innocent and righteous thou shalt not slay; thou shalt not justify the wicked; and thou shalt not take a gift, for gifts blind the eyes of them that see and pervert righteous words." Of this divine law, then, Moses, who also was God's servant, was made the minister both to all the world, and chiefly to the Hebrews, who were also called Jews, whom an Egyptian king had in ancient days enslaved, and who were the righteous seed of godly and holy men—Abraham, and Isaac, and Jacob. God, being mindful of them, and doing marvelous and strange miracles by the hand of Moses, delivered them, and led them out of Egypt, leading them through what is called the desert; whom He also settled again in the land of Canaan, which afterwards was called Judea, and gave them a law, and taught them these things. Of this great and wonderful law, which tends to all righteousness, the ten heads are such as we have already rehearsed.

CHAPTER X.—OF HUMANITY TO STRANGERS.

Since therefore they were strangers in the land of Egypt, being by birth Hebrews from the land of Chaldæa,—for at that time, there being a famine, they were obliged to migrate to Egypt for the sake of buying food there, where also for a time they sojourned; and these things befell them in accordance with a prediction of God,—having sojourned, then, in Egypt for 430 years, when Moses was about to lead them out into the desert, God taught them by the law, saying, "Ye shall not afflict a stranger; for ye know the heart of a stranger: for yourselves were strangers in the land of Egypt."

CHAPTER XI.—OF REPENTANCE.

And when the people transgressed the law which had been given to them by God, God being good and pitiful, unwilling to destroy them, in addition to His giving them the law, afterwards sent forth also prophets to them from among their brethren, to teach and remind them of the contents of the law, and to turn them to repentance, that they might sin no more. But if they persisted in their wicked deeds, He forewarned them that they should be delivered into subjection to all the kingdoms of the earth; and that this has already happened them is manifest. Concerning repentance, then, Isaiah the prophet, generally indeed to all, but expressly to the people, says: "Seek ye the Lord while He may be found, call ye upon Him while He is near: let the wicked forsake his ways, and the unrighteous man his thoughts: and let him return unto the Lord his God, and he will find mercy, for He will abundantly pardon." And another prophet, Ezekiel, says: "If the wicked will turn from all his sins that he hath committed, and keep all My statutes, and do that which is right in My sight, he shall surely live, he shall not die. All his transgressions that he hath committed, they shall not be mentioned unto him; but in his righteousness that he hath done he shall live: for I desire not the death of the sinner, saith the Lord, but that he turn from his wicked way, and live." Again Isaiah: "Ye who take deep and wicked counsel, turn ye, that ye may be saved." And another prophet, Jeremiah: "Turn to the Lord your God, as a grape-gatherer to his basket, and ye shall find mercy." Many therefore, yea rather, countless are the sayings in the Holy Scriptures regarding repentance, God being always desirous that the race of men turn from all their sins.

CHAPTER XII.—OF RIGHTEOUSNESS.

Moreover, concerning the righteousness which the law enjoined, confirmatory utterances are found both with the prophets and in the Gospels, because they all spoke inspired by one Spirit of God. Isaiah accordingly spoke thus: "Put away the evil of your doings from your souls; learn to do well, seek judgment, relieve the oppressed, judge the fatherless, plead for the widow." And again the same prophet said: "Loose every band of wickedness, dissolve every oppressive contract, let the oppressed go free, and tear up every unrighteous bond. Deal out thy bread to the hungry, and bring the houseless poor to thy home. When thou seest the naked, cover him, and hide not thyself from thine own flesh. Then shall thy light break forth as the morning, and thine health shall spring forth speedily, and thy righteousness shall go before thee." In like manner also Jeremiah says: "Stand in the ways, and see, and ask which is the good way of the Lord your God, and walk in it and ye shall find rest for your souls. Judge just judgment, for in this is the will of the Lord your God." So also says Hosea: "Keep judgment, and draw near to your God, who established the heavens and created the earth." And another, Joel, spoke in agreement with these: "Gather the people, sanctify the congregation, assemble the elders, gather the children that are in arms; let the bridegroom go forth of his chamber, and the bride out of her closet, and pray to the Lord thy God urgently that he may have mercy upon you, and blot out your sins." In like manner also another, Zachariah: "Thus saith the Lord Almighty, Execute true judgment, and show mercy and compassion every man to his brother; and oppress not the widow, nor the fatherless, nor the stranger; and let none of you imagine evil against his brother in your heart, saith the Lord Almighty."

CHAPTER XIII.—OF CHASTITY.

And concerning chastity, the holy word teaches us not only not to sin in act, but not even in thought, not even in the heart to think of any evil, nor look on another man's wife with our eyes to lust after her. Solomon, accordingly, who was a king and a prophet, said: "Let thine eyes look right on, and let thine eyelids look straight before thee: make straight paths for your feet." And the voice of the Gospel teaches still more urgently concerning chastity, saying: "Whosoever looketh on a woman who is not his own wife, to lust after her, hath committed adultery with her already in his heart." "And he that marrieth," says [the Gospel], "her that is divorced from her husband, committeth adultery; and whosoever putteth away his wife, saving for the cause of fornication, causeth her to commit adultery." Because Solomon says: "Can a man take fire in his bosom, and his clothes not be burned? Or can one walk upon hot coals, and his feet not be burned? So he that goeth in to a married woman shall not be innocent."

CHAPTER XIV.—OF LOVING OUR ENEMIES.

And that we should be kindly disposed, not only towards those of our own stock, as some suppose, Isaiah the prophet said: "Say to those that hate you, and that cast you out, Ye are our brethren, that the name of the Lord may be glorified, and be apparent in their joy." And the Gospel says: "Love your enemies, and pray for them that despitefully use you. For if ye love them who love you, what reward have ye? This do also the robbers and the publicans." And those that do good it teaches not to boast, lest they become men pleasers. For it says: "Let not your left hand know what your right hand doeth." Moreover, concerning subjection to authorities and powers, and prayer for them, the divine word gives us instructions, in order that "we may lead a quiet and peaceable life." And it teaches us to render all things to all, "honor to whom honor, fear to whom fear, tribute to whom tribute; to owe no man anything, but to love all."

CHAPTER XV.—THE INNOCENCE OF THE CHRISTIANS DEFENDED.

Consider, therefore, whether those who teach such things can possibly live indifferently, and be commingled in unlawful intercourse, or, most impious of all, eat human flesh, especially when we are forbidden so much as to witness shows of gladiators, lest we become partakers and abettors of murders. But neither may we see the other spectacles, lest our eyes and ears be defiled, participating in the utterances there sung. For if one should speak of cannibalism, in these spectacles the children of Thyestes and Tereus are eaten; and as for adultery, both in the case of men and of gods, whom they celebrate in elegant language for honors and prizes, this is made the subject of their dramas. But far be it from Christians to conceive any such deeds; for with them temperance dwells, self-restraint is practiced, monogamy is observed, chastity is guarded, iniquity exterminated, sin extirpated, righteousness exercised, law administered, worship performed, God acknowledged: truth governs, grace guards, peace screens them; the holy word guides, wisdom teaches, life directs, God reigns. Therefore, though we have much to say regarding our manner of life, and the ordinances of God, the maker of all creation, we yet consider that we have for the present reminded you of enough to induce you to study these things, especially since you can now read [our writings] for yourself, that as you have been fond of acquiring information, you may still be studious in this direction also.

CHAPTER XVI.—UNCERTAIN CONJECTURES OF THE PHILOSOPHERS.

But I wish now to give you a more accurate demonstration, God helping me, of the historical periods, that you may see that our doctrine is not modern nor fabulous, but more ancient and true than all poets and authors who have written in uncertainty. For some, maintaining that the world was uncreated, went into infinity; and others, asserting that it was created, said that already 153,075 years had passed. This is stated by Apollonius the Egyptian. And Plato, who is esteemed to have been the wisest of the Greeks, into what nonsense did he run? For in his book entitled *The Republic*, we find him expressly saying: "For if things had in all time remained in their present arrangement, when ever could any new thing be discovered? For ten thousand times ten thousand years elapsed without record, and one thousand or twice as many years have gone by since some things were discovered by Dædalus, and some by Orpheus, and some by Palamedes." And when he says that these things happened, he implies that ten thousand times ten thousand years elapsed from the flood to Dædalus. And after he has said a great deal about the cities of the world, and the settlements, and the nations, he owns that he has said these things conjecturally. For he says, "If then, my friend, some god should promise us, that if we attempted to make a survey of legislation, the things now said," etc., which shows that he was speaking by guess; and if by guess, then what he says is not true.

CHAPTER XVII.—ACCURATE INFORMATION OF THE CHRISTIANS.

It behoved, therefore, that he should the rather become a scholar of God in this matter of legislation, as he himself confessed that in no other way could he gain accurate information than by God's teaching him through the law. And did not the poets Homer and Hesiod and Orpheus profess that they themselves had been instructed by Divine Providence?

Moreover, it is said that among your writers there were prophets and prognosticators, and that those wrote accurately who were informed by them. How much more, then, shall *we* know the truth who are instructed by the holy prophets, who were possessed by the Holy Spirit of God! On this account, all the prophets spoke harmoniously and in agreement with one another, and foretold the things that would come to pass in all the world. For the very accomplishment of predicted and already consummated events should demonstrate to those who are fond of information, yea rather, who are lovers of truth, that those things are really true which they declared concerning the epochs and eras before the deluge: to wit, how the years have run on since the world was created until now, so as to manifest the ridiculous mendacity of your authors, and show that their statements are not true.

CHAPTER XVIII.—ERRORS OF THE GREEKS ABOUT THE DELUGE.

For Plato, as we said above, when he had demonstrated that a deluge had happened, said that it extended not over the whole earth, but only over the plains, and that those who fled to the highest hills saved themselves. But others say that there existed Deucalion and Pyrrha, and that they were preserved in a chest; and that Deucalion, after he came out of the chest, flung stones behind him, and that men were produced from the stones; from which circumstance they say that men in the mass are named "people." Others, again, say that Clymenus existed in a second flood. From what has already been said, it is evident that they who wrote such things and philosophized to so little purpose are miserable, and very profane and senseless persons. But Moses, our prophet and the servant of God, in giving an account of the genesis of the world, related in what manner the flood came upon the earth, telling us, besides, how the details of the flood came about, and relating no fable of Pyrrha nor of Deucalion or Clymenus; nor, forsooth, that only the plains were submerged, and that those only who escaped to the mountains were saved.

CHAPTER XIX.—ACCURATE ACCOUNT OF THE DELUGE.

And neither does he make out that there was a second flood: on the contrary, he said that never again would there be a flood of water on the world; as neither indeed has there been, nor ever shall be. And he says that eight human beings were preserved in the ark, in that which had been prepared by God's direction, not by Deucalion, but by Noah; which Hebrew word means in English "rest," as we have elsewhere shown that Noah, when he announced to the men then alive that there was a flood coming, prophesied to them, saying, Come thither, God calls you to repentance. On this account he was fitly called Deucalion. And this Noah had three sons (as we mentioned in the second book), whose names were Shem, and Ham, and Japhet; and these had three wives, one wife each; each man and his wife. This man some have surnamed Eunuchus. All the eight persons, therefore, who were found in the ark were preserved. And Moses showed that the flood lasted forty days and forty nights, torrents pouring from heaven, and from the fountains of the deep breaking up, so that the water overtopped every high hill 15 cubits. And thus the race of all the men that then were was destroyed, and those only who were protected in the ark were saved; and these, we have already said, were eight. And of the ark, the remains are to this day to be seen in the Arabian mountains. This, then, is in sum the history of the deluge.

CHAPTER XX.—ANTIQUITY OF MOSES.

And Moses, becoming the leader of the Jews, as we have already stated, was expelled from the land of Egypt by the king, Pharaoh, whose name was Amasis, and who, they say, reigned after the expulsion of the people 25 years and 4 months, as Manetho assumes. And after him [reigned] Chebron, 13 years. And after him Amenophis, 20 years 7 months. And after him his sister Amessa, 21 years 1 month. And after her Mephres, 12 years 9 months. And after him

Methramuthosis, 20 years and 10 months. And after him Tythmoses, 9 years 8 months. And after him Damphenophis, 30 years 10 months. And after him Orus, 35 years 5 months. And after him his daughter, 10 years 3 months. After her Mercheres, 12 years 3 months. And after him his son Armais, 30 years 1 month. After him Messes, son of Miammus, 6 years, 2 months. After him Rameses, 1 year 4 months. After him Amenophis, 19 years 6 months. After him his sons Thoessus and Rameses, 10 years, who, it is said, had a large cavalry force and naval equipment. The Hebrews, indeed, after their own separate history, having at that time migrated into the land of Egypt, and been enslaved by the king Tethmosis, as already said, built for him strong cities, Peitho, and Rameses, and On, which is Heliopolis; so that the Hebrews, who also are our ancestors, and from whom we have those sacred books which are older than all authors, as already said, are proved to be more ancient than the cities which were at that time renowned among the Egyptians. And the country was called Egypt from the king Sethos. For the word Sethos, they say, is pronounced "Egypt." And Sethos had a brother, by name Armais. He is called Danaus, the same who passed from Egypt to Argos, whom the other authors mention as being of very ancient date.

CHAPTER XXI.—OF MANETHO'S INACCURACY.

And Manetho, who among the Egyptians gave out a great deal of nonsense, and even impiously charged Moses and the Hebrews who accompanied him with being banished from Egypt on account of leprosy, could give no accurate chronological statement. For when he said they were shepherds, and enemies of the Egyptians, he uttered truth indeed, because he was forced to do so. For our forefathers who sojourned in Egypt were truly shepherds, but not lepers. For when they came into the land called Jerusalem, where also they afterwards abode, it is well known how their priests, in pursuance of the appointment of God, continued in the temple, and there healed every disease, so that they cured lepers and every unsoundness. The temple was built by Solomon the king of Judæa. And from Manetho's own statement his chronological error is manifest. (As it is also in respect of the king who expelled them, Pharaoh by name. For he no longer ruled them. For having pursued the Hebrews, he and his army were engulphed in the Red Sea. And he is in error still further, in saying that the shepherds made war against the Egyptians.) For they went out of Egypt, and thenceforth dwelt in the country now called Judæa, 313 years before Danaus came to Argos. And that most people consider him older than any other of the Greeks is manifest. So that Manetho has unwillingly declared to us, by his own writings, two particulars of the truth: first, avowing that they were shepherds; secondly, saying that they went out of the land of Egypt. So that even from these writings Moses and his followers are proved to be 900 or even 1000 years prior to the Trojan War.

CHAPTER XXII.—ANTIQUITY OF THE TEMPLE.

Then concerning the building of the temple in Judæa, which Solomon the king built 566 years after the exodus of the Jews from Egypt, there is among the Tyrians a record how the temple was built; and in their archives writings have been preserved, in which the temple is proved to have existed 143 years 8 months before the Tyrians founded Carthage (and this record was made by Hiram (that is the name of the king of the Tyrians), the son of Abimalus, on account of the hereditary friendship which existed between Hiram and Solomon, and at the same time on account of the surpassing wisdom possessed by Solomon. For they continually engaged with each other in discussing difficult problems. And proof of this exists in their correspondence, which to this day is preserved among the Tyrians, and the writings that passed between them); as Menander the Ephesian, while narrating the history of the Tyrian kingdom, records, speaking thus: "For when Abimalus the king of the Tyrians died, his son Hiram succeeded to the kingdom. He lived 53 years. And Bazorus succeeded him, who lived 43, and reigned 17 years. And after him followed Methuastartus, who lived 54 years, and reigned 12. And after him succeeded his brother Atharymus, who lived 58 years, and reigned 9. He was slain by his brother of the name of Helles, who lived 50 years, and reigned 8 months. He was killed by Juthobalus, priest of Astarte, who lived 40 years, and reigned 12. He was succeeded by his son Bazorus, who lived 45 years, and reigned 7. And to him his son Metten succeeded, who lived 32 years, and reigned 29. Pygmalion, son of Pygmalius succeeded him, who lived 56 years, and reigned 7. And in the 7th year of his reign, his sister, fleeing to Libya, built the city which to this day is called Carthage." The whole period, therefore, from the reign of Hiram to the founding of Carthage, amounts to 155 years and 8 months. And in the 12th year of the reign of Hiram the temple in Jerusalem was built. So that the entire time from the building of the temple to the founding of Carthage was 143 years and 8 months.

CHAPTER XXIII.—PROPHETS MORE ANCIENT THAN GREEK WRITERS.

So then let what has been said suffice for the testimony of the Phoenicians and Egyptians, and for the account of our chronology given by the writers Manetho the Egyptian, and Menander the Ephesian, and also Josephus, who wrote the Jewish war, which they waged with the Romans. For from these very old records it is proved that the writings of the rest are more recent than the writings given to us through Moses, yes, and than the subsequent prophets. For the last of the prophets, who was called Zechariah, was contemporary with the reign of Darius. But even the lawgivers themselves are all found to have legislated subsequently to that period. For if one were to mention Solon the Athenian, he lived in the days of the kings Cyrus and Darius, in the time of the prophet Zechariah first mentioned, who was by many years the last of the prophets. Or if you mention the lawgivers Lycurgus, or Draco, or Minos, Josephus tells us in his writings that the sacred books take precedence of them in antiquity, since even before the reign of Jupiter over the Cretans, and before the Trojan war, the writings of the divine law which has been given to us through Moses were in existence. And that we may give a more accurate exhibition of eras and dates, we will, God helping us, now give an account not only of the dates after the deluge, but also of those before it, so as to reckon the whole number of all the years, as far as possible; tracing up to the very beginning of the creation of the world, which Moses the servant of God recorded through the Holy Spirit. For having first spoken of what concerned the creation and genesis of the world, and of the first man, and all that happened after in the order of events, he signified also the years that elapsed before the deluge. And I pray for favor from the only God, that I may accurately speak the whole truth according to His will, that you and every one who reads this work may be guided by His truth and favor. I will then begin first with the recorded genealogies, and I begin my narration with the first man.

CHAPTER XXIV.—CHRONOLOGY FROM ADAM.

Adam lived till he begat a son, 230 years. And his son Seth, 205. And his son Enos, 190. And his son Cainan, 170. And his son Mahaleel, 165. And his son Jared, 162. And his son Enoch, 165. And his son Methuselah, 167. And his son Lamech, 188. And Lamech's son was Noah, of whom we have spoken above, who begat Shem when 500 years old. During Noah's life, in his 600th year, the flood came. The total number of years, therefore, till the flood, was 2242. And immediately after the flood, Shem, who was 100 years old, begat Arphaxad. And Arphaxad, when 135 years old, begat Salah. And Salah begat a son when 130. And his son Eber, when 134. And from him the Hebrews name their race. And his son Phaleg begat a son when 130. And his son Reu, when 132 And his son Serug, when 130. And his son Nahor, when 75. And his son Terah, when 70. And his son Abraham, our patriarch, begat Isaac when he was 100 years old. Until Abraham, therefore, there are 3278 years. The fore-mentioned Isaac lived until he begat a son, 60 years, and begat Jacob. Jacob, till the migration into Egypt, of which we have spoken above, lived 130 years. And the sojourning of the Hebrews in Egypt lasted 430 years; and after their departure from the land of Egypt they spent 40 years in the wilderness, as it is called. All these years, therefore, amount to 3,938. And at that time, Moses having died, Jesus the sun of Nun succeeded to his rule, and governed them 27 years. And after Jesus, when the people had transgressed the commandments of God, they served the king of Mesopotamia, by name Chusarathon, 8 years. Then, on the repentance of the people, they had judges: Gothonoel, 40 years; Eglon, 18 years; Aoth, 8 years. Then having sinned, they were subdued by strangers for 20 years. Then Deborah judged them 40 years. Then they served the Midianites 7 years. Then Gideon judged them 40 years; Abimelech, 3 years; Thola, 22 years; Jair, 22 years. Then the Philistines and Ammonites ruled them 18 years. After that Jephthah judged them 6 years; Esbon, 7 years; Ailon, 10 years; Abdon, 8 years. Then strangers ruled them 40 years. Then Samson judged them 20 years. Then there was peace among them for 40 years. Then Samera judged them one year; Eli, 20 years; Samuel, 12 years.

CHAPTER XXV.—FROM SAUL TO THE CAPTIVITY.

And after the judges they had kings, the first named Saul, who reigned 20 years; then David, our forefather, who reigned 40 years. Accordingly, there are to the reign of David [from Isaac] 496 years. And after these kings Solomon reigned, who also, by the will of God, was the first to build the temple in Jerusalem; he reigned 40 years. And after him Rehoboam,
17 years; and after him Abias, 7 years; and after him Asa, 41 years; and after him Jehoshaphat, 25 years; and after him Joram, 8 years; and after him Ahaziah, 1 year; and after him Athaliah, 6 years; and after her Josiah, 40 years; and after him Amaziah, 39 years; and after him Uzziah, 52 years; and after him Jotham, 16 years; and after him Ahaz, 17 years; and after him Hezekiah, 29 years; and after him Manasseh, 55 years; and

after him Amon, 2 years; and after him Josiah, 31 years; and after him Jehoahaz, 3 months; and after him Jehoiakim, 11 years. Then another Jehoiakim, 3 months 10 days; and after him Zedekiah, 11 years. And after these kings, the people, continuing in their sins, and not repenting, the king of Babylon, named Nebuchadnezzar, came up into Judæa, according to the prophecy of Jeremiah. He transferred the people of the Jews to Babylon, and destroyed the temple which Solomon had built. And in the Babylonian banishment the people passed 70 years. Until the sojourning in the land of Babylon, there are therefore, in all, 4954 years 6 months and 10 days. And according as God had, by the prophet Jeremiah, foretold that the people should be led captive to Babylon, in like manner He signified beforehand that they should also return into their own land after 70 years. These 70 years then being accomplished, Cyrus becomes king of the Persians, who, according to the prophecy of Jeremiah, issued a decree in the second year of his reign, enjoining by his edict that all Jews who were in his kingdom should return to their own country, and rebuild their temple to God, which the fore-mentioned king of Babylon had demolished. Moreover, Cyrus, in compliance with the instructions of God, gave orders to his own bodyguards, Sabessar and Mithridates, that the vessels which had been taken out of the temple of Judæa by Nebuchadnezzar should be restored, and placed again in the temple. In the second year, therefore, of Darius are fulfilled the 70 years which were foretold by Jeremiah.

CHAPTER XXVI.—CONTRAST BETWEEN HEBREW AND GREEK WRITINGS.

Hence one can see how our sacred writings are shown to be more ancient and true than those of the Greeks and Egyptians, or any other historians. For Herodotus and Thucydides, as also Xenophon, and most other historians, began their relations from about the reign of Cyrus and Darius, not being able to speak with accuracy of prior and ancient times. For what great matters did they disclose if they spoke of

Darius and Cyrus, barbarian kings, or of the Greeks Zopyrus and Hippias, or of the wars of the Athenians and Lacedæmonians, or the deeds of Xerxes or of Pausanias, who ran the risk of starving to death in the temple of Minerva, or the history of Themistocles and the Peloponnesian war, or of Alcibiades and Thrasybulus? For my purpose is not to furnish mere matter of much talk, but to throw light upon the number of years from the foundation of the world, and to condemn the empty labor and trifling of these authors, because there have neither been twenty thousand times ten thousand years from the flood to the present time, as Plato said, affirming that there had been so many years; nor yet 15 times 10,375 years, as we have already mentioned Apollonius the Egyptian gave out; nor is the world uncreated, nor is there a spontaneous production of all things, as Pythagoras and the rest dreamed; but, being indeed created, it is also governed by the providence of God, who made all things; and the whole course of time and the years are made plain to those who wish to obey the truth. Lest, then, I seem to have made things plain up to the time of Cyrus, and to neglect the subsequent periods, as if through inability to exhibit them, I will endeavor, by God's help, to give an account, according to my ability, of the course of the subsequent times.

CHAPTER XXVII.—ROMAN CHRONOLOGY TO THE DEATH OF M. AURELIUS.

When Cyrus, then, had reigned twenty-nine years, and had been slain by Tomyris in the country of the Massagetæ, this being in the 62d Olympiad, then the Romans began to increase in power, God strengthening them, Rome having been founded by Romulus, the reputed child of Mars and Ilia, in the 7th Olympiad, on the 21st day of April, the year being then reckoned as consisting of ten months. Cyrus, then, having died, as we have already said, in the 62d Olympiad, this date falls 220 A.U.C., in which year also Tarquinius, surnamed Superbus, reigned over the Romans, who was the first who banished Romans and corrupted the youth, and made eunuchs of the citizens, and, moreover, first defiled virgins, and then gave them in marriage. On this account he was fitly called Superbus in the Roman language, and that is translated "the Proud." For he first decreed that those who saluted him should have their salute acknowledged by some one else. He reigned twenty-five years. After him yearly consuls were introduced, tribunes also and ediles for 453 years, whose names we consider it long and superfluous to recount. For if any one is anxious to learn them, he will ascertain them from the tables which Chryserus the nomenclator compiled: he was a freedman of Aurelius Verus, who composed a very lucid record of all things, both names and dates, from the rounding of Rome to the death of his own patron, the Emperor Verus. The annual magistrates ruled the Romans, as we say, for 453 years. Afterwards those who are called emperors began in this order: first, Caius Julius, who reigned 3 years 4 months 6 days; then Augustus, 56 years 4 months 1 day; Tiberius, 22 years; then another Caius, 3 years 8 months 7 days; Claudius, 23 years 8 months 24 days; Nero, 13 years 6 months 58 days; Galba, 2 years 7 months 6 days; Otho, 3 months 5 days; Vitellius, 6 months 22 days; Vespasian, 9 years 11 months 22 days; Titus, 2 years 22 days; Domitian, 15 years 5 months 6 days; Nerva, 1 year 4 months 10 days; Trajan, 19 years 6 months 16 days; Adrian, 20 years 10 months 28 days; Antoninus, 22 years 7 months 6 days; Verus, 19 years 10 days. The time therefore of the Cæsars to the death of the Emperor Verus is 237 years 5 days. From the death of Cyrus, therefore, and the reign of Tarquinius Superbus, to the death of the Emperor Verus, the whole time amounts to 744 years.

CHAPTER XXVIII.—LEADING CHRONOLOGICAL EPOCHS.

And from the foundation of the world the whole time is thus traced, so far as its main epochs are concerned. From the creation of the world to the deluge were 2242 years. And from the deluge to the time when Abraham our forefather begat a son, 1036 years. And from Isaac, Abraham's son, to the time when the people dwelt with Moses in the desert, 660 years. And from the death of Moses and the rule of Joshua the son of Nun, to the death of the patriarch David, 498 years. And from the death of David and the reign of Solomon to the sojourning of the people in the land of Babylon, 518 years 6 months 10 days. And from the government of Cyrus to the death of the Emperor Aurelius Verus, 744 years. All the years from the creation of the world amount to a total of 5698 years, and the odd months and days.

CHAPTER XXIX.—ANTIQUITY OF CHRISTIANITY.

These periods, then, and all the above-mentioned facts, being viewed collectively, one can see the antiquity of the prophetical writings and the divinity of our doctrine, that the doctrine is not recent, nor our tenets mythical and false, as some think; but very ancient and true. For Thallus mentioned Belus, king of the Assyrians, and Saturn, son of Titan, alleging that Belus with the Titans made war against Jupiter and the so-called gods in his alliance; and on this occasion he says that Gyges, being defeated, fled to Tartessus. At that time Gyges ruled over that country, which then was called Acte, but now is named Attica. And whence the other countries and cities derived their names, we think it unnecessary to recount, especially to you who are acquainted with history. That Moses, and not he only, but also most of the prophets who followed him, is proved to be older than all writers, and than Saturn and Belus and the Trojan war, is manifest. For according to the history of Thallus, Belus is found to be 322 years prior to the Trojan War. But we have shown above that Moses lived somewhere about 900 or 1000 years before the sack of Troy. And as Saturn and Belus flourished at the same time, most people do not know which is Saturn and which is Belus. Some worship Saturn, and call him Bel or Bal, especially the inhabitants of the eastern countries, for they do not know who either Saturn or Belus is. And among the Romans he is called Saturn, for neither do they know which of the two is more ancient—Saturn or Bel. So far as regards the commencement of the Olympiads, they say that the observance dates from Iphitus, but according to others from Linus, who is also called Ilius. The order which the whole number of years and Olympiads holds, we have shown above. I think I have now, according to my ability, accurately discoursed both of the godlessness of your practices, and of the whole number of the epochs of history. For if even a chronological error has been committed by us, of, e.g., 50 or 100, or even 200 years, yet not of thousands and tens of thousands, as Plato and Apollonius and other mendacious authors have hitherto written. And perhaps our knowledge of the whole number of the years is not quite accurate, because the odd months and days are not set down in the sacred books. But so far as regards the periods we speak of, we are corroborated by Berosus, the Chaldæan philosopher, who made the Greeks acquainted with the Chaldæan literature, and uttered some things concerning the deluge, and many other points of history, in agreement with Moses; and with the prophets Jeremiah and Daniel also, he spoke in a measure of agreement. For he mentioned what happened to the Jews under the king of the Babylonians, whom he calls Abobassor, and who is called by the Hebrews Nebuchadnezzar. And he also spoke of the temple of Jerusalem; how it was desolated by the king of the Chaldæans, and that the foundations of the temple having been laid the second year of the reign of Cyrus, the temple was completed in the second year of the reign of Darius.

CHAPTER XXX.—WHY THE GREEKS DID NOT MENTION OUR HISTORIES.

But the Greeks make no mention of the histories which give the truth: first, because they themselves only recently became partakers of the knowledge of letters; and they themselves own it, alleging that letters were invented, some say among the Chaldæans, and others with the Egyptians, and others again say that they are derived from the Phoenicians.

And secondly, because they sinned, and still sin, in not making mention of God, but of vain and useless matters. For thus they most heartily celebrate Homer and Hesiod, and the rest of the poets, but the glory of the incorruptible and only God they not only omit to mention, but blaspheme; yes, and they persecuted, and do daily persecute, those who worship Him. And not only so, but they even bestow prizes and honors on those who in harmonious language insult God; but of those who are zealous in the pursuit of virtue and practice a holy life, some they stoned, some they put to death, and up to the present time they subject them to savage tortures. Wherefore such men have necessarily lost the wisdom of God, and have not found the truth. If you please, then, study these things carefully, that you may have a compendium and pledge of the truth.

www.ingramcontent.com/pod-product-compliance
Lightning Source LLC
Chambersburg PA
CBHW052111070526
44584CB00017B/2431